CONCILIUM

CONCILIUM 2006/5

THE RESURRECTION OF THE DEAD

Edited by
Andrés Torres Queiruga
Luiz Carlos Susin
Jon Sobrino

SCM Press · London

Published by SCM Press, 9–17 St Albans Place, London N1 0NX

Copyright © Stichting Concilium

English translations copyright © 2006 SCM-Canterbury Press Ltd

All rights reserved. No part of this publication may be
reproduced, stored in a retrieval system, or transmitted,
in any form or by any means, electronic, mechanical, photocopying,
recording or otherwise, without the prior written permission of
Stichting Concilium, Erasmusplein 1,
6525 HT Nijmegen, The Netherlands

ISBN 0 334 03091 9

Printed and bound in Great Britain by
William Clowes Ltd, Beccles, Suffolk

Concilium published February, April, June, October
December

Contents

Introduction
ANDRÉS TORRES QUEIRUGA, LUIZ CARLOS SUSIN,
JON SOBRINO   7

I. The Religious Common Ground   13

Death and its Religious 'Management' in Human History
KARL-HEINZ OHLIG   15

Dying and Rising Again in a Popular Tradition
DIEGO IRARRAZAVAL   25

On Dying Hard: Lessons from Popular Crucifixions and Undisciplined Resurrections in Latin America
MARCELLA MARIA ALTHAUS-REID   35

II. The Specifically Christian Vision   45

Resurrection in the Israelite Tradition
SENÉN VIDAL   47

Jesus Raised as 'Primrose' of Shared Resurrection
GIUSEPPE BARBAGLIO   56

Metaphysical Aspects of the Concept of Resurrection
THOMAS SCHÄRTL   65

III. Resurrection in Present Life   79

The Resurrection of Nature: an Aspect of Cosmic Christology
    JÜRGEN MOLTMANN   81

Resurrection as Process of a New Life
    MÁRCIO FABRI DOS ANJOS   90

The Resurrection of One Crucified: Hope and a Way of Living
    JON SOBRINO   100

Resurrection and Funeral Liturgy
    ANDRÉS TORRES QUEIRUGA   110

I Believe in Resurrection
    PEDRO CASALDÁLIGA   121

Conclusion: Resurrection: the Heart of Life and Faith
    LUIZ CARLOS SUSIN   125

Documentation

I. Migration from Africa to Spain
    RAFAEL LARA   131

II. Migration from Latin America to North America
    ALBERTO LOPEZ PULIDO   135

Contributors   138

Introduction

ANDRÉS TORRES QUEIRUGA, LUIZ CARLOS SUSIN, JON SOBRINO

Speaking of resurrection means speaking of the biblical tradition and especially of the Christian tradition. Christ is the Risen One *par excellence*, to the point where it is common to find the most specific mark of Christianity in this proclamation. The resurrection is in fact its way of facing up to one of the great questions of humankind, perhaps *the* question: what becomes of us after death, what awaits us or what can we hope for after this dark and inexorable abyss? And what effects does answering one way or another have on our present life?

It is understandable that the resurrection should have become one of the major concerns of present-day theology. From occupying a few paragraphs, or at most a few brief pages, in the manuals, its study has multiplied in quantity and variety. From being reduced to a 'miracle', perhaps the greatest and most spectacular but ultimately an event in this world used for 'apologetic purposes', it has moved to the centre of Christology and has begun to be considered truly in itself, in its intrinsic significance and its renewing potentiality for life and history. As a result, articles, monographs, and conferences on the subject have multiplied – a change that can only be welcomed with joy and hope.

Nevertheless, the task cannot be considered finished. There has been a great advance both in overall focus and in realization of its importance, as there has been above all in the study of the historical and exegetical details. Viewing this in historical terms, however, shows it to be a still very recent change, and one that has been weighed down with strong resistance from those who are fearful that renewal *in the manner* of understanding it will do away with the actual *content* of the truth: that *theology of it* will become a threat to *faith in it*. The very weight of a venerable tradition and sometimes also the inertia of theological routines have led to an ongoing lack of appreciation of the depth and consequences of the exegetical and historical studies, as of the advances made by a profoundly renewed hermeneutics.

As a result, there still remains ample space for re-structuring the overall imagery and conceptual formulations within the current cultural climate, taking account primarily of the deep break brought about by Modernity and of the increasingly intense and effective meeting with other religious traditions. This issue of *Concilium* – like past ones such as 1993/5, edited by Hermann Häring and Johann-Baptist Metz, and 1991/4, edited by Metz and Edward Schillebeeckx – seeks to contribute to the joint and open task of authentic updating on the subject.

There is a need, in the first place, to profit from the distancing from biblical fundamentalism, left behind on principle after long and hard resistance to it, with timid beginnings in the seventeenth century, but which has still not borne all its fruits in theological practice. The nature of the narratives, written by witnesses who were neither present at the original events nor the first to reflect on them; their late and geographically removed development; their not directly historical but rather kerygmatic and catechetical purpose of nourishing faith; their symbolic language, combined with irreconcilable discrepancies in times, persons, and places – all these factors oblige us to re-read these narratives, seeking to recover, beyond their *text*, their *spirit*, the underlying intention that informs them. There is no doubt that these are *theological* narratives that testify to a deep experience of *faith*, expressed through the linguistic, inventive, and conceptual resources available to them at the time.

We must not, then, feel confined by a text that deserves all our attention and respect but whose authentic message cannot be rescued on the basic of making formal adjustments or superficial amendments. What is needed is a determined hermeneutical overturning, aimed at recovering the 'world' (Ricoeur) opened up by the texts, abandoning the fascination of continuing to take them as 'narrations' of actual events. This, which should lead to the re-configuration of a mental approach largely formed by and modelled on literary narrations and iconographic representations, will help to liberate our thinking and enable us to concentrate on the basic problems and consequences.

So this issue opens with a setting of the resurrection in the general framework of the religious and even cultural history of the human race. Today it would be unforgivable to ignore the concern for dialogue with other religions. The new receptivity to their traditions (and their cultures) keeps alive the need to include resurrection in the *humus* of the 'religious common ground' of humankind, avoiding the danger of seeing it as a sort of 'meteorite' deprived of intelligibility through lack of any true grounding in the *humanum*. Furthermore, in this way, dialogue has become truly fraternal and essentially open, trying not only to get to know other religions, but also to learn from them those aspects that their culture and tradition alone can make intelligible as part of the deep mystery that God has for all time been trying to reveal to us all. There is space in this issue of *Concilium* to study only a few of them, but the articles here can serve as examples and models for further studies. In any case we have thought it right not to confine ourselves to dialogue with Hellenism, since today dialogue not only with the East but also with the ancestral traditions of Africa and Latin America (the only example taken into account here) has become indispensable.

Within the religious common ground, the specifically Christian vision, very much taking account of the results of contemporary exegesis, concentrates on clarifying the basic lines that marked the advance of biblical thought in its passage from Old Testament to New Testament. It has become increasingly clear to us that on crucial points exegetical discussion leaves the question of historical factualness in a *non liquet*, which can be genuinely discussed only by being very conscious of the basic hermeneutical options, which in turn refer us to the new cultural situation.

On all these grounds, taking the radical depth of the cultural change seriously has become a main concern. Theological reflection today has to keep on high alert against not just an ingenuously biological view of the resurrection (luckily largely discarded), but above all an insufficiently cautious conception in the face of the positivist temptation, which tends to interpret the accounts of the appearances and the empty tomb as ultimately 'physical' proofs.

Far from putting the reality of the resurrection in danger, this caution underlines its *transcendent nature*, which does not reduce but emphasizes and testifies to the glorification of the Risen Christ, his 'exaltation', which raises him above the limitations of the empirical laws that would imprison him within the narrow limits of space and time. It is precisely on this nature that the reality and effectiveness of his universal presence is founded, on the basis of his identification with the Father in the power of the Spirit.

In passing, the problem of 'verification' of the resurrection is situated on its rightful level, which is more demanding in both epistemological and religious terms, but freed from the empiricist traps that, as in the case of the 'invisible gardener', make faith impossible, by unreasonably requiring physical proofs of a transcendent reality.

Only in this way will it be possible for a real and contemporary dialogue to take place with a *culture* that, rightly, views the discovery of the autonomy of natural laws to be irreversible. Taking it into account can be seen to constitute a decisive pre-condition when we come to study the problem and unpack the meaning of the narratives concerning the appearances and the empty tomb.

From this it follows that the very possibility of the concept of resurrection needs to be submitted to a careful examination, given its deep implication in the metaphysical and linguistic problems whose resolution intensely preoccupies thought today. This is something equally reflected, on a more lively and basic level, in concerns to discover – *sub contrario*, as it were – new ways and fashions of experiencing resurrection, as expressed in demonstrations such as protest crucifixions: beyond their possible ambiguities, they help people to understand the deep realism of resurrection, as it was revealed in the destiny of Christ who was crucified and raised.

This leads on to the attention that must be paid to the praxic aspect, which demands that we insist on the inexorable need to place the victims at the heart of any Christian interpretation of the resurrection. This is first and foremost for the real and present hope of those men and women whom human injustice or simply natural circumstances have united more directly and painfully to the fate of Christ crucified. But it is also for all the others, who will only in this way be able to *believe* in the resurrection without lying, thereby beginning in history a life that, through expressing committed solidarity with the victims, does not betray but advances the raising power of the Lord in life on earth. This has to be the authentic root of any Christic and Christian sense that would not betray the decisive lesson of Jesus of Nazareth. By going back to its roots in this way, it simultaneously tunes in with one of the noblest concerns of present-day refection on the meaning of history: 'the longing for the executioner not to triumph over the victim'.

The praxic dimension in itself points to the ecological concern and cosmic reach essentially implied in Christian insistence on the resurrection *of the flesh*. Corporeal and not angelic beings, men and women live and develop in strict solidarity with nature. Our eschatological hope should in some mysterious fashion include material creation, so that the resurrection, far form any escapism, becomes a dynamic force renewing and reconciling an earth that through human beings is also going through 'the pains of childbirth' on its way to the ultimate fullness.

The Church celebrates the hope of this fullness intensely and constantly in each individual death, which arrives with the light of Christ's resurrection and indissolubly linked to his destiny. Freed from concern over its miraculous nature and exclusivity, the resurrection shows Jesus as the true 'firstborn among the dead', not in a merely chronological sense but in the

Introduction

deepest, most universal sense of ultimate revelation; that is, revelation of that which, essentially, 'at many times and in many ways', the God of the living has been trying to reveal from the start through the eschatological hope that, with greater or lesser clarity, has been and is palpable in all religions.

Far from watering down or blurring the richness and even the originality of the biblical and Christian concept of resurrection, the new approaches confirm these, shedding light on them from the different perspectives that inform the work of present-day theology. This work is done in solidarity with other religions, in no spirit of competition or exclusiveness but providing a friendly exchange and welcoming their contributions, as it does the deepest insights of those cultural concerns that seek new paths towards the future of the human race. Once more, as on so many occasions in history, the challenge of change, accepted in honesty and with concern for clarity, is a summons to effort (and perhaps a degree of hesitation), but it can become a genuine *kairós*, which can make the luminous mystery of the Pasch of the risen Christ shine with new tints.

The editors would like to thank the following for their suggestions for this issue: Marcella Althaus-Reid, Edward Farrugia, Rosino Gibellini, Harry McSorley, David Power, Elaine Wainwright.

I. The Religious Common Ground

Death and its Religious 'Management' in Human History

KARL-HEINZ OHLIG

I. The inevitable end

Human beings are the only forms of life that are aware that they will die. What is more, they see death as an utterly predictable outcome. At certain points in life, to be sure, we are quite able to blank out this fact occasionally, or to allow it to recede somewhat into the background. But consideration of death and of the fear it induces constantly catches up with us, and then it is capable of calling in question life as a whole, with all its commitments and ties. To that extent, 'being unto death' (Martin Heidegger) is an appropriate description not, indeed, of the events and phases of human life but of its fundamental structure.

Human history shows that death has never been a fact merely known and acknowledged. It has always been treated as an ultimate threat, since it involves final separation from loved ones or the end of one's own life. Death is a challenge to the meaningfulness of human existence.

Admittedly, there are certain critical situations in which death appears desirable as a form of 'deliverance'. But this is the case only if definite instances of suffering, such as torture or physical or mental illness, make death seem a form of escape and liberation. In such cases the actual critical juncture 'obscures' the perception of death as menace without abrogating this, its basic, characteristic.

In religions of whatever kind we encounter a holistic interpretation of human existence, and therefore of history and of the 'world' and of what is perceived in them partially. Accordingly, the prospect of death plays a central role in all of them. It is impossible to attribute meaning to humankind without integrating death in that meaning, and simultaneously 'managing' or 'coping with it' in some way.

Almost all, apart from some Semitic, religions offer their followers a form of hope beyond death and accept that there is a 'life after death'. They express this hope in their myths, in ritual accompaniments of burials and of other forms of committal of the dead, and, in more sophisticated religions, by means of ethical norms for a life lived in awareness of death.

In the history of religion we meet with this hope in a 'life after death' in the most differentiated forms and notional worlds, and in various degrees of intensity. Nevertheless, it is a constantly recurrent theme that has only recently been called in question by individuals or small groups that seek to come to terms with the as yet inexplicably fragmentary nature of life.

II. Testimonies from the history of religion[1]

(a) Prehistory

Some 2.6 million years ago the human species emerged from the transitional area between animals and humans. More than two million years of this history are shrouded in obscurity. We (still?) know nothing about the religious ideas of that stretch of time, and therefore nothing about their attitude to death. In early millennia religion must have been expressed only in rudimentary practices (rites, dances, and behaviour patterns) that have left no traces over vast tracts of time. If only in a purely abstract sense, we may assume that forms of life which – even if in small steps lasting for millennia – began to develop what we might term 'culture' were concerned about themselves and also about the 'end'; about, that is, death. Occasionally we meet with the suggestion that the archaeological discoveries of buried crania reaching back to early millennia are (also) to be ascribed to separate treatment during burials, and that this phenomenon might indicate associated religious concepts, although nothing is certain in this regard.

There have been (still) very sparse finds of skulls assignable to dates over about the last 500,000 years and showing partial traces of ritual handling (a pierced occiput), as well as similarly dated longer bones that have been split, both probably treated thus to allow brains and marrow to be eaten (ritual cannibalism). These discoveries at least show clearly that dead people were handled and buried differently (to animals, that is); and that, therefore, their death was perceived as a problem that required ritual treatment of the corpse and associated interpretation of it as a means of 'overcoming' death. Occasional finds of red ochre, which at a later date was an unambiguous symbol of blood and thus of (new) life, most probably also indicate that life for the dead was anticipated and was something to be induced ritually.

From the middle Stone Age, since about 100,000 years ago, there have been numerous discoveries of burial sites from across the world that show unmistakably that people were interred in accordance with ritual rules intended to express hope of a life after death. The bodies were usually buried in an east-west orientation (the 'axis of life'), and often crouching (perhaps indicating a return to the numinous maternal womb to be reborn); sometimes together with other ritual remains (traces of pollen from wreaths of flowers, circles of stones or of horns, and so on), and often with specks of red ochre. It is also possible that adjacent stone objects, especially hearth-stones, were put there to help the dead in their future life.

We know nothing of any ideas associated with survival beyond death. There is reason to think that the model from which humans derived the notion of life after death was the observed natural cycle of sunrise and nightfall and of birth, death, and new life rising from the earth's womb. But once this view of things was associated with actual dead people, an additional element pointed beyond the merely vegetative understanding of death: hope was placed in an extension of life for this particular dead individual, not merely in further generations of human beings.

Numerous burials are known from the early Palaeolithic era, in Europe from 40,000 BC, that offer the possibility of more precise deductions. Dead people were buried with their clothing on a layer of red ochre, or were strewn with ochre. They were interred in different physical attitudes, often pointing in obviously intended directions; the skulls were often treated separately. For the first time unmistakable objects chosen to accompany the dead were present, usually jewellery and stone equipment. At that time ideas and myths regarding death and its significance must have been scattered all over the world, but we know nothing of them (the extremely great distance in time between then and now makes attempts to reconstruct these concepts from comparisons with recent hunting and food-gathering cultures questionable by the standards of historico-critical analysis). Nevertheless, the type of ritual remains encountered, especially red-ochre instances, indicates belief in a 'life after death' and obviously in one in which clothes, ornaments, and tools would be needed. The veneration of the numinous womb of the earth that was practised all over the world at that time, especially as found in the treatment of caves and in numerous statuettes of steatopygous women, shows that a kind of rebirth was an accepted belief. These forms of burial are also to be found in the Mesolithic Age, from 12,000 BC (known, in the case of extra-European cultures, as the Epipalaeolithic era).

The Neolithic age, from 9000 BC, represents a decisive break in human development and was the basis of the later rise of advanced cultures. The transition to cultivation and cattle-raising (the 'Neolithic revolution') made possible a higher density of population, a form of social differentiation (warrior caste, priests, artisans, farmers, nomadic shepherds), and life in villages and towns. This was when the human being finally became *homo faber* and was no longer passively oriented to whatever nature offered to be collected and hunted.

From this point on, a regional cultural differentiation began to take effect. Nevertheless certain constants were still effective all over the world. The numinous was still conceived of objectively, hereafter in the sense of simultaneously fruitful and threatening natural processes, although the anthropomorphic features of, say, female statuettes were more emphatic, and the numinous powers were often venerated in sanctuaries erected by human beings.

From now on burial rites vary in different cultures. But they all show that it is accepted that the dead live on. The forces of fruitfulness are effective in death, just as they are in the vegetative world. But the interpretation of death and rebirth in accordance with the models provided by the processes of vegetation would seem to afford only the basis for conceiving the life after death of specific dead persons, for quite often 'individual' characteristics are also recognizable (for instance, gender-specific committals, imitation of facial features, burial below a living-space, and, in many cultures, the practice of ancestor-worship). The objects buried with the corpse (vessels containing food, ochre deposits, jewellery for women and weapons for men) make sense only if the new life was conceived along the lines of the old one. And then the graves in some Neolithic cultures contain 'soul holes' to allow the souls of the dead free passage.

(b) Concepts of the soul and the 'management' of death

The occasional provision of 'soul holes' in late Stone Age burials, especially in the Megalithic culture, shows that the assumption that there was such a thing as a human soul would seem to have arisen then, to have remained effective in later advanced cultures, and to have continued to take effect in our contemporary world religions. In association with burials, this means that there was awareness of the different nature of 'life after death'. Obviously the body decays, so that the 'identity' of the individual surviving death could be guaranteed only by another, that is, by a non-corporeal, reality.

We do not know what notions were specifically attached to 'soul holes', yet the minimal diameter of these apertures shows that whatever aspect of a human being lives on or is reborn has nothing to do with his or her physical dimensions. The images of burial objects sometimes found on the walls of graves indicate something similar: 'We may see this as indicating the surrender of purely material notions, as is evident . . . in the transition from actual objects placed in graves to their mere portrayal on the walls of graves.'[2] Similarly, the fact that the burial objects in many Neolithic cultures were smashed beforehand could indicate that they were no longer intended to be 'really' used. Whether the incineration of the dead and the burial of the ashes more frequently practised from now on are to be understood in the same context cannot be decided with any certainty, since even later there is a constantly recurring interchange of burials and incinerations, the specific reasons for which are unknown.

Whatever name it goes by, the soul is always an invisible and therefore a human reality that is not, in the normal sense, physical. To assume its existence makes it easier to believe that 'some aspect of a human being' survives during the process of changing to a new life. Of course for the most part predictive images of this transition are conceived in terms of the ever-new successive periods apparent in nature, which offer constantly changing shapes. To the fore in this conception, in the ages under consideration, was the continually renewed succession of birth, death, and rebirth in vegetation, plants, and animals. The new life arising in this development does indeed depend on its origin in reproductive processes, or from seed, but new forms of life do come into being in nature that are not at all 'identical' with the originating forms. The seed-corn dies so that new life can develop. Accordingly, the idea of a soul appears to be a supportive construction which allows one to conceive of a continuing life of an actual human being beyond the natural process in which people and their death are embedded. The concept of souls is intended to declare that the seed-corn does not merely die, but lives on – though its form has changed.

An extremely wide variety of later concepts of the soul is recorded in advanced cultures. There are ideas of only a *single* soul – sometimes because of the simplicity of a particular culture, but also for highly-nuanced reasons. There are also notions of *several* souls, when either different human functions are hypostatized to become souls (a spiritual, physical, and intellectual soul), or different relations determine plurality: the ancestors live on in a soul; a soul is transferred to descendants; another ensures the 'individuality' of a person; and so forth.

A common feature of all these concepts is the idea that this human reality is (or that these human realities are) not merely physical. But they often remain attached to the corpse, as in the case of the 'soul holes'. These do not serve only to enable the soul to move on but allow it constantly to return to the body. Similarly, in, for instance, the religion of ancient Egypt, the continued existence of the soul is dependent on the survival of the corpse, which for that reason was mummified at great expense. This reference to the onetime corporeal reality of a dead person was retained in the later form of Christian theology influenced by Hellenism. Accordingly, in spite of its natural immortality, the soul is the form – or innermost reality – of the body, and its existence up to the point of 'resurrection' is one of relationship to its body.

Later on, the soul is conceived of as immaterial in principle, as 'spirit', in only a few cultures. It is often thought of as a kind of 'attenuated materiality', so that souls need 'holes' in order to leave graves. The North African theologian Tertullian (d. after 220) even portrayed God himself as a kind of gaseous physicality.[3] That is also the reason why even generally accepted concepts of the soul did not always rule out the inclusion of real objects to accompany the buried corpse, as is shown, for example, by the libation pipes in Roman graves, which were to be used to feed the dead.

In general, concepts of the soul take into account the scarcely negligible fact that dead bodies rot (or are burnt), and often, when some time has passed, nothing is left of them. In this respect, however different and diffuse they may be individually, they provide a basis for expressing the survival of specific human beings beyond death.

(c) Advanced religions

Advanced cultures and religions from 3000 BC feature the first literary pronouncements on death and its significance. These not only take the form of explicit descriptions of a 'life after death' but occur in the – numerous – creation myths with their directly or indirectly anthropological statements.

The most important change from previous eras was the personalization of the numinous powers as gods and goddesses. The resulting pantheons were usually subject to patriarchal government but differed considerably from one culture to another, with varying numbers, functions and degrees of individualization of the deities. Nevertheless, the new tendency to personal divinities also allowed the individual particularity of human beings to emerge more emphatically, and in many, if not all, advanced religions they had to assume religious and moral responsibility for their lives and answer for their conduct to personal tribunals, which usually meant a divine Judge. In these religions the significance of this present historical life extends to the next world (the judgment of the dead), though sometimes, as with the Aztecs, only with regard to the mode of death.

Nevertheless, as creation myths throughout the world demonstrate, the powers of nature take precedence over, or are set above, the gods, for the divinities themselves emerged from the chaotic forces of nature in self-generated motion (the 'very beginning') – probably a notion inherited from prehistoric concepts of creation – and their activity is subject to an irrefragable natural law.

This thematic complex gives rise to a number of different views of what lies beyond death. All advanced religions, apart from certain Semitic instances, 'defeat' the threat of death by proposing various notions of the soul. Then death is not final but merely a *transition* to a new life in a different form.

In some advanced religions the essential difference of the life led by the soul is not to the fore, or, as in the Rig-Veda, it is assumed that the soul will have a new body, and these religions anticipate a happy afterlife – though not always for everyone. This afterlife is conceived of analogously to the present one: for example, on an 'isle of the blessed' (as in Celtic religion); in a martial paradise (as in Germanic religion); or at all events in satisfying association with one's ancestors (the most ancient Vedic concepts).

Not a few advanced religions, however, feature a continued existence of the soul alone in a 'shadowy realm' that offers a somewhat dreary prospect for survivors. There is often no mention of how long this 'life after death' might last, and people are satisfied to assume that it will be a long stretch. But in other cultures the continued existence of individuals is associated with posterity's memories of them, or with the (sacrificial) gifts that descendants dedicate to their forebears. Accordingly their individual existence fades, for example, after three generations within the confines of Chinese cultures, and after five generations in Africa (except for monarchs and heroes).

In some religions (the Celtic, for instance, and later Vedic and Greek) we find the idea of a rebirth of the soul (in another person), or of a migration of souls – a notion that probably comes from observation of the cycle of plant growth and of the fact that human life is often brutally cut short by death when it has not yet been 'lived to the full'.

A few Semitic religions fail to 'cope with' or 'overcome' death by positing an afterlife; instead they see death as the definitive end of human life. This is connected with the relevant cultures' supreme orientation to history and not to natural processes, and with their tendency to interpret humankind historically and not quasi-organologically; and human beings viewed historically terminate with death. Nevertheless, here too we find some 'attempts to nullify death', in, for instance, the protocanonical writings of the Old Testament where hope is placed in plenteous descendants, the possession of territory, or the future of the people – a version that is of help only insofar as individuals still conceive of themselves predominantly in a 'collective' sense, as parts of an ethnic group. In the Babylonian-Assyrian Gilgamesh epic, for example, the hero acknowledges the definitive nature of death and busies himself in accomplishing great works and cultural achievements in which he will 'live on'.

(d) Universal religions

From 3000 BC, as highly-advanced religions evolved further, concepts that posited a universal religious significance applicable in principle to every human being emerged in dynamic regions. Monistic and monotheistic religions are the two major and diametrically opposed groups of variants on this theme.

Monistic religions conceive of the horizon, or limits, of things in objectively divine terms, and propose as an aim the abrogation of any division between humans and this 'god' resulting from their separate historical existence (or 'duality'). Therefore they look forward to self-transcendence in the unity of the divine. This is the goal of universal concepts in Hellenism (mystery cults and 'philosophical' schools) and in Chinese schemata of this kind (Taoism, and to some extent also Confucianism). The universal theories of Hinduism based on Vedic tradition (the theology of the Upanishads, schools of Vedantic philosophy) and Buddhism take up the traditional notion of cyclic rebirths and look to their termination and a simultaneous self-transcendence in 'the One' by means of a form of transcension of karma, or destiny, and therefore of any existential tie to history, so that there is no longer any reason for rebirth.

The monotheistic religions (Judaism, Christianity, and Islam), on the other hand, trust in the eternal persistence of each individual with God. It was a long time before the notion of a 'reawakening'/'resurrection' developed in the Jewish religion, from which Christianity and Islam received this belief. This particular theme occurs for the first time only in early Judaism, in the time of the Maccabees. Initially – as in the literature of the Deuterocanonical books (or, as Reformed usage generally has it, the Apocrypha) of the Old Testament – there is reference only to a resurrection of the just. This prospect is extended to 'everyone' only in inter-Testament literature and in the New Testament.

III. Summary

Insofar as we can decipher the testimonies of the history of religion, the frightening prospect of death was 'overcome' by hope of life after death, however such a life was conceived. This hope took a visible form in burial rites; with the development of advanced cultures, in myths recorded in literary forms; and also, in highly-nuanced religions, by the ethical constitution of life in view of eventual death.

Recourse to the idea of a soul makes it easier to cope with death. This soul is understood as an 'existential' or 'natural' something that survives death. To some extent, connected as it is with the many instances of 'changing forms' in nature, this notion helps people to liberate death from the terror it awakens in them. Then it is no longer 'just the end and no more' but 'merely' a *transitus*, or transition, of one and the same soul from one state to another.

The idea of 'resurrection' that arose in early Judaism and was reinforced in the New Testament is not a 'natural' construction that makes it much easier to deal with death, which remains the unresolved end of an historical existence and does not shed its terror. Nevertheless, this particular conception does articulate a form of hope reaching beyond the barrier represented by death. It is a hope for which only images are available: of a dead person lying there as if asleep who is 'awakened' and 'rises' to his or her feet again. This metaphorical discourse relies on hope of divine activity in this respect, and not on any form of existential evidence.

This conception both takes death seriously and dispenses with mythic justifications. Nevertheless, at an early date it ceased to hold its ground in Christianity and, by derivation from Christianity, in Islam. Even from early on in the post-New Testament period, this hope of resurrection was associated with traditional Hellenistic ideas of a naturally immortal soul. As in certain other religions, it seemingly resolved the threat of death, and made a life after death appear rationally acceptable. But this apparently plausible idea was still based on a mythic thought process.

Translated by J. G. Cumming

Notes

1. Cf. in this respect, K.-H. Ohlig, ¹2002, ²2006, *Religion in der Geschichte der Menschheit. Die Entwicklung des religiösen Bewusstseins*, Darmstadt.
2. J. Maringer, 1956, *Vorgeschichtliche Religion*, Zürich, p. 270 (Eng. trans. *The Gods of Prehistoric Man*, 1960, London].
3. Tertullian portrayed the spiritual substance of God and of the soul as 'a form of matter that is invisible though not wholly intangible' (K.-H. Ohlig, 1986, *Fundamentalchristologie. Im Spannungsfeld von Christentum und Kulture*, Munich, p. 194; see also A. Grillmeier, 1979, *Jesus Christus im Glauben der Kirche*, vol. I: *Von der Apostolischen Zeit bis zum Konzil von Chalkedon*, Freiburg, Basle and Vienna, pp. 243, 255).

Dying and Rising Again in a Popular Tradition

DIEGO IRARRAZABAL

Just as death is both adorned and hidden in developed societies, resurrection is similarly disregarded. Going to a funeral is seen as a waste of time. The idea that we die and rise again(!) is treated with contempt. Most people build up a mass of transient and superficial pastimes and have lost touch with stately and communal celebrations. This devastating de-humanization has been spread and partly assimilated throughout the planet.

In the Americas and on other continents, however, there are good persistent traditions that reconstruct modernity. Contact with 'the living dead' is a common denominator in little and great civilizations across the globe. The inhabitants of Latin America, especially the indigenous peoples, face up to death well and also – in their own way – to the new life.

In general, the rites and festivities associated with those who have died are humanizing. Furthermore, they show many signs of 'fullness of life', through sharing with friends and family members and with neighbours. As for Christian spirituality, it includes a feeling for the Crucified Christ as the one who empowers the humble, and a feeling for God on feast-days. These and other day-to-day experiences bring a re-appreciation of the resurrection of Jesus Christ and of humankind. Furthermore, through dialogue with 'other' cultures and with autonomous and syncretic forms of religion, Latin American theologies are re-stating understanding of salvation in Christ.[1]

The Latin American approach is neither ingenuous nor dispassionate. 'The question resurrection poses is whether we too share in the scandal of bringing death to the righteous, whether we are on the side of the killers or on the side of the God who gives life': that is, resurrection is understood as from the crucified people, as Jon Sobrino has pointed out.[2] This affects everyone, since not only do the powerful oppress the weak, but the poor too discriminate among themselves. Each person can opt for the God who gives life.

I hear Paul's question, 'How are the dead raised?' echo in my ears, and the lucid paradox: 'It is sown in weakness, it is raised in power. It is sown a physical body, it is raised a spiritual body' (1 Cor. 15.35, 43–4). Catholic teaching accepts that the Spirit of God offers everyone (and not only those who believe what we do) the chance of being taken up in the paschal mystery (GS 22) and, through the grace of God, called to salvation (LG 13). This is a beautiful mystery, and it transforms the Andean peoples.

I. An original people that dies and rises again

Despite discrimination and fragmentation, indigenous peoples of Latin America (some fifty million souls, with varied cultures and contexts) make their passion for life in its fullness manifest. Everyday reality – summed up in oral and ritual tradition – provides many signs of resurrection. A superficial reading suggests that these local cultures have spirituality but would be lacking in soteriology and that their piety has more of Good Friday than of Easter Sunday.

A good way to start is by recognizing signs – of faith in resurrection – in daily love of neighbour, in veneration of the earth, in experiencing death. In Peru and Bolivia there are one-and-a-half million modern Andean-Aymara and innumerable mixed-race people; these communities are re-configuring indigenous ways. I am here summarizing what has been described by various writers, and what I have appreciated and celebrated.[3]

We need to consider both their pre-Hispanic origins and their survival over the centuries. In 1621 Pablo Joseph de Aliaga noted the following: 'In the death and burial of their deceased they have great abuses and superstitions; they usually dress them in new clothes under their shrouds . . . and when they do them the honours, they place boiled and roast meats on their tombs so that they may eat, even though this is forbidden . . . and they say that in church the dead are weighed down painfully with earth, and that in the country, as they are in the open air and not buried, they rest more easily'.[4] Still today one can see the Aymara people (and Quechua, Maya, and others) giving food to their dead-living. They go on burying them in cultivated plots where their ancestors rest and now watch over their lives. So there is a cosmic understanding of living-dying.

For the present theme of resurrection, the widespread practice of companionship around recently deceased persons is significant. At the beginning of November (All Saints and All Souls days) family members and friends come together to strengthen bonds. They prepare and ritually offer the favourite dishes and drinks of each deceased. There is a sequence of speeches, dialogues, banquets, prayers, rites of welcome and farewell to the

Dying and Rising Again in a Popular Tradition

'soul' (who arrives on November 1st and leaves on the 2nd). There is also a human and sacred fellowship on the first anniversaries – a month, a year, and three years after the death. These customs are changing to suit circumstances and places, and substitutes (a quick, modern funeral) are beginning to take their place.

As for beliefs, their attitudes to old people and very young children are significant. Someone who has lived well and for a long time dies 'as God wishes' and is a well-celebrated soul (as opposed to those who die 'punished' for a wickedness they have committed and who are condemned for their social and moral irresponsibility). Children, for their part, are considered 'little angels'; people trust that God will take them and make them happy, and their death is met with a measured response. So there is series of actions that symbolically marry death to life. When they feel death approaching, Aymara give advice to their survivors, and this marks the behaviour of the new generations ('I do what I was told' by a grandfather, wife, husband, and so on). The concerns of the dying go on to become guidelines for living well.

The cycle of death, vigil, and burial has its own profound language, with overtones of resurrection. There are lit candles and flowers around the corpse, to whom people pray because it is present there. Select persons wash and lay out the body for its 'journey' to rest. Over intense nights and days, the dead person and those who live on are well 'accompanied' (because to leave them on their own would be a crime). Around death, food and drink are shared generously. Other signs of life are making the sign of the cross, praying the Our Father and Hail Mary, using holy water, singing hymns, praying the rosary, and other Catholic actions inculturated into Aymara death – putting a cross on the coffin and the tomb; ritual offerings of earth, flowers, and other elements of life on top of and inside the coffin; a ceremonial salutation to the corpse, which listens to and accepts various signs of life together; similar salutations among those present, who also share drinks and sometimes food.

Then comes the cycle of commemoration. Eight or nine days after the death a fresh all-night vigil is held. Clothes are washed, and there are ceremonies in the house and at the place of burial. The belief is that deceased persons are starting out on a journey towards where dead people live next to God. Since they are travelling, things that will be useful on the journey are placed on the coffin, and the dead are told to give counsel and greetings to those who have died earlier. After a month, three months, six months, then a year (depending on family and social circumstances), social gatherings are held. There are rites in church and at the burial ground (whether this is an important plot of agricultural land or the local cemetery). The dead person is present and spoken of and with. 'Responses' are prayed and food prepared and shared (especially at the beginning of November, as already noted). The 'souls' depart satisfied, and the family too feel at peace and protected by the ancestors and by all renowned dead persons. Yet there are also signs of apprehension and fear: dead people send one signs when one dreams of them; they sometimes punish and cause misfortunes; they have to be placated through rituals.

These indigenous practices and beliefs persist today, with modifications and admixtures. They require interpretation both from within the sensitivity and wisdom of the humble of the earth (a first way) and from the social sciences (a second way). That first way understands customs from within, with their cosmic and historical spirituality and their non-western logic. The second way (a scientific understanding) tends to leave aside the spiritual aspect, which in indigenous thinking is inseparable from all worldly matters, but it does provide analytical explanations and relates various factors: family, economic, psycho-social, and others. All of this challenges faith reflection and goes on to form part of it: theology does not float above historical processes but is rather developed within the ways of dying and living proper to every nation.

II. Polychromatic approach: interpretations

If we are to understand the Andean approach to death, we need to immerse ourselves in this non-western reality. When what the inhabitants experience is interpreted by non-indigenous observers such as myself,[5] our cultural and spiritual categories have to be used with great caution; this can be with both empathy and a critical approach, and we need to avoid one-sided preconceptions derived from a particular philosophy or science or theology. Furthermore, the indigenous population today moves in several worlds and is largely multicultural. All this both complicates and adds to the interest of efforts to understand polychromatic experiences of the Aymara in particular and autochthonous peoples in general.

Allow me to stress that in Latin America autochthonous does not indicate something archaic and exotic, since the original communities inter-marry and reconstruct modernity according to the autochthonous paradigm of relatedness. We therefore need to study and tune in to intercultural and polysemic ways of living.

A first hermeneutical approach: the indigenous world-view is basically oriented to life that includes death. The life-force of the universe is expressed in Aymara by the concept of *jacana* and in Quechua by *kawsay*. So we are dealing with an all-inclusive view, in which life and death are 'complementary, meta-individual, cosmic' aspects (José Estermann). Following this approach, resurrection can be envisaged not as what happens to the individual *post-mortem* but rather as personal fullness in a cosmic, collective, transcendent reality. This implies appreciating the human race and creation, which form part of the risen body of Christ.

A second line of interpretation: the autochthonous outlook 'takes on cultural and religious elements, intermingling and syncretizing them, but without diluting their identity' (J. Van Kessel). In family and community, new life springs from death, as opposed to the secular view of the cycle from birth to death. We might ask whether Christian reflection takes up and completes this autochthonous faith. Unfortunately, it tends to be disqualified by personalist philosophies or by the dualism in which one reality does not include another different from it.

Another line of enquiry: to recognize Christ in the journey of a people, so making his message relevant to the original culture. In Bolivia they regard the 'cosmic cross' (with its twenty or twenty-eight sides), and in Central America they see the 'pan-Amerindian cross', as having Christ at their heart and centre. Enrique Jordá understands the Aymaran and also the Mesoamerican experience as God's alliance with the human race; he sees the resurrection of Jesus who died on the cross as the centre of the universe that unites God with the new humanity, as the origin of our hope, and as sharing in the birth for which all creation is longing.

Recently (in church meetings set up by CELAM in Mexico, Mesoamerica, and other parts of the continent), indigenous representatives have been asked how they see Christ. This is as a '*buar*', the main beam in the houses of the Kuna people of Panamá; or as '*Bagará*', the liberator of the Embera people; or as personal saviour in Ngobe culture (both also of Panamá/Darien); or as suffering and risen among the indigenous peoples of El Salvador; or as 'Word of God made flesh who is growing in the Mayan world with their own vigour and expression' (as indicated by the Catholic bishops of Guatemala).

So far I have dealt with present-day interpretations from an inculturated standpoint. Nevertheless, during the centuries of colonialism and then in modern indoctrination and fundamentalist versions, autochthonous and *mestizo* spirituality and wisdom have been discounted. One controversial case is the Evangelical campaign among the Qom/Toba peoples of

Argentina (examined by Aldana and Bruno; n. 5). 'The crucifixion of Qom cosmogony has been the death of their culture . . . and resurrection was preached as the capacity to understand and adapt to the (western) Christian mission.' Similar cultural and spiritual crimes have been committed by other Christian missions (sometimes in subtle ways but equally destructive of the indigenous soul). This needs to be evaluated ecclesially and theologically.

Works dealing with indigenous ways of life show them to be highly complex and polychromatic. In contemporary indigenous experiences, which are assailed by impoverishment and discrimination, the essential is to affirm Life from the framework of family, community, cosmos, and history. In short: relatedness is what 'saves' the fragile entities of the universe. This can be interpreted in terms of a 'pan-zoism', of the community factor that includes the personal, and also of the cosmic factor that forms part of the history of salvation.

III. Rising-on-death and salvation in Christ

Theological endeavour presupposes that human experiences (and in this case indigenous ones) are addressed by Christian revelation and that this is grasped by the *sensus fidei* of the people. What stands out here is the indigenous understanding of rising-on-death, on which I make four comments.

The first of these refers to fidelity to revelation. According to the New Testament, rising in Christ has meaning both during earthly life and after death. 'Just as Christ was raised from the dead . . . so we too might walk in newness of life' (Rom. 6.4); 'he who raised Christ from the dead will give life to your mortal bodies also through his Spirit that dwells in you' (Rom. 8.11). As a result, the indigenous community questions itself on its shared life with the Risen Christ and on the passage from physical death to life in fullness. This applies to all human existence and its transcendence, and it also applies to the cosmos, clamouring for its liberation.

When the indigenous community defines itself as Christian, it questions itself on its relationship to the deceased on the basis of their relationship to Christ. Christians cultivate their relationship to Christ, who died crucified but who lives because God did not allow evil to triumph over life. So then, this 'real and unique relationship', as Andrés Torres Queiruga calls it, is the foundational model for 'relationship with the dead . . . with them too there exists a relationship of real presence here and now, of communion and interchange'.[6] This can be seen at work in the indigenous and mixed-race population of America.

My second comment is the Latin American way of looking at the crucified Jesus. Reflection has placed the accent on the kingdom of God, which is life for the poor. Jesus of Nazareth proclaimed and brought about the kingdom of God for marginalized people. The poor are the crucified/raised to life of yesterday and today. This is the source of a reading of the subject of resurrection that is not universalizing but incarnate. In an analogous manner to the kingdom being destined for the poor, the resurrection is understood precisely in relation to the crucified people. Those who are crucified today provide 'a privileged viewpoint for understanding the resurrection of Jesus in a Christian spirit'.[7] Because of this the indigenous community does not, in its manner of living the faith, spiritualize either the kingdom or the resurrection.

Third comment: testimonies that nourish faith. Contemporary exegesis and theology have been re-reading the apparition narratives and the subject of the tomb. These matters, when we engage in philosophical dialogue with modern culture, are viewed in a manner neither empiricist nor as demonstration of a truth via a miracle. More value is placed on the testimony of those who believe that the love of God has raised the crucified Christ to life. That is, the risen Christ is recognized through a faith experience and not because the laws of time and space have been set aside.

This is relevant to beliefs of any age and culture. For instance, it is relevant to the indigenous beliefs in fellowship with the deceased (on the first days of November each year). An empiricist reading would say that this is false or pure fantasy. Another reading of such a testimony to faith might admire the human sensitivity, the *sensus fidei*, and the Andean theology it demonstrates – which does not involve sacralizing each and every indigenous custom.

The community constantly asks to what extent it is showing an evangelical adherence to the risen Christ in these beliefs. Adherence is evangelical when it is accompanied by signs of love of neighbour and of genuine trust in the God of life. The ritual (ceremonies for families and visitors, offerings to the dead person, and so on) is evaluated according to these criteria. Testimony of faith in the risen Christ is expressed in ritual, in the framework of the indigenous passage from death to life, or rather, of rising-on-dying.

A fourth comment: indigenous theological exploration. My first comment was on faithfulness to revelation; this inevitably contains inculturated features. Being a disciple today implies a love in the form of service throughout life and when this passes through death. Indigenous and mixed-race communities do not normally explain their faith in the risen Christ verbally, but they do so in ritual and symbolically with rich non-verbal expressions. Community and creation groan for their salvation. So I am stressing that the Christian event is relevant to this people in all their personal, cosmic, historical concerns.

We may ask: What criteria exist for verifying whether the existence of the crucified people is in fact transformed? The New Testament explains the experience of faith in terms of liberation and joy. This characterizes the experience of the disciples, men and women. Being free 'is justified from resurrection' and 'in spite of everything and contrary to everything, following the crucified Christ brings its own joy'.[8] Is this how it is in the Aymara communities? When do the crucified people cultivate hope, instead of assimilating the daily racial and cultural discrimination and violence? In contexts where there is so much *machismo* and subordination of women, we need to look for signs of new men and new women.

A fifth and final point: my use of the concept 'living-on-dying' is informed both by indigenous symbols in Latin America and by the notion of 'living dead' in African societies. There are distinct expressions that share inculturation of faith in the God of Life and manifestation of aspects of salvation in Christ. '[T]he Holy Spirit, in a manner known only to God, offers to [all] the possibility of being associated with this paschal mystery' (GS 22, taken up by John Paul II in RM 10). It can then be said that, besides inculturations with Christian cultural imprints, there are 'non-western' ways of envisaging resurrection. Aymara customs and understandings (condensed in rites surrounding death) can be understood as a rising-on-dying. It is a soteriology that faces up to their daily crucifixion and that underpins modes of love as service.

Various regions of the world set forth routes to salvation that marry life and death.[9] In Mexico and throughout the American continent there is 'an intense network of relationships that bind the community of the living to their dead . . . in popular Latin American circles every death implies a special reactivation of the community around the family of the deceased'. In African societies there is also a warm relationship with the 'living dead', who, according to John Mbiti, 'go on being persons' and are 'the best intermediaries between human beings and God'. Michael Kirwen describes the living dead as showing that 'death is passing to the life beyond, since the spirits of the dead continue living'. In Asia cosmic and meta-cosmic beliefs complement one another, according to Alonso Pieris, who accepts as 'a fresh source of revelation for the Church in Asia' not only what is known through Christian categories but also 'the religious sense of the poor of Asia, the majority of whom are non-Christian'. We can then appreciate that each symbolic structure holds death to be not the last word but a radical crisis that confirms life.

Conclusion

A population whose life paradigm is indigenous and mixed-race (and which keeps a degree of autonomy in relation to Christianities from the West) invites us now to re-read the mystery of the resurrection in a cosmic and historical manner. This re-reading stems from a relational paradigm in which dying goes hand in hand with being raised, in which the relationship with the dead evokes symbols of cosmic fullness, and in which each actual community is reactivated around death. The population of Latin America and of other regions of the world is the bearer of its own rites and interpretations of resurrection. The Saviour of the world is the first-born of all those who die (see Rev. 1.17). In a preferential way he is that of today's crucified people: impoverished and migrant multitudes in cities, original nations, discriminated-against minorities. Just as God raised his crucified Son, the same happens with those subjected to violence today. Evil does not crush us. Life conquers in the people and creation all around us.

Translated by Paul Burns

Notes

1. See various, 2003, ⁴2006, *Por los muchos caminos de Dios*, vols. I–IV, Quito: Abya Yala.
2. J. Sobrino, 1982, *Jesús en América Latina*, Santander: Sal Terrae, p. 238 (Eng. trans., *Jesus in Latin America*, Maryknoll, NY: Orbis, 1984). See also L. Boff, 1986, *La resurrección de Cristo. Nuestra resurrección en la muerte*, Santander: Sal Terrae; M. Faijó, X. Alegre, A. Tornos, 1998, *La fe cristiana en la resurrección*, Santander: Sal Terrae.
3. See V. Ochoa, 1975, *Entierro y ritos a los difuntos*, Chucuito: Boletín IDEA; W. Carter and M. Mamani, 1982, *Irpa chico. Individuo y comunidad en la cultura aymara*, La Paz: Juventud, pp. 329–69; D. Llanque, 1990, *La cultura aymara*, Lima: Tarea, pp. 109–10; X. Albó, 'La experiencia religiosa aymara', in various, 1991, *Rostros indios de Dios*, Quito: Abya Yala, pp. 232–35; J. van Kessel, 1999, *Los vivos y los muertos, duelo y ritual mortuorio en los Andes*, Iquique: IECTA; J. Estermann, 2006, *Filosofía andina*, La Paz: ISEAT, pp. 231–36; J. Quispe, 2006, *Hacia una ecoteología*, Cochabamba:ILM-UCB. On other cultures: M. S.

Cipoletti and E. J. Langdon, 1992, *La muerte y el más allá en las culturas indígenas latinoamericanas*, Quito: Abya Yala; H.-C. Puech, 1982, 'Almas de los muertos y mundo de los vivos', in *Las religiones en los pueblos sin tradición escrita*, Mexico City, Siglo XXI.
4. J. J. de Arriaga, 1999, *La extirpación de la idolatría en el Piru, 1621*, Cuzco: CBC, pp. 66–7.
5. I am using interpretations by J. van Kessel, *op. cit.*; J. Estermann, *op. cit.*; E. Jordá, 2006, *Cristo en el Titikaka*, unpublished, p. 82. On other indigenous worldviews: S. Aldana and D, Bruno, 2005, *Cruz y resurrección para una teología india. Memoria del III encuentro regional México y Centroamérica*, Bogotá: CELAM, pp. 98, 100, 110, 133, 144.
6. A. Torres Queiruga, 2005, *Repensar la resurrección*, Madrid: Trotta, pp. 284, 328.
7. J. Sobrino, *Jesús*, p. 236.
8. *Idem*, pp. 246–7.
9. See J. L. González, 2002, *Fuerza y sentido. El catolicismo popular al comienzo del siglo XXI*, Mexico City: Dabar, p. 119; J. Mbiti, 1969, *African Religions and Philosophy*, Nairobi: Heinemann, p. 83; M. Kirwen, 2005, *African Cultural Knowledge*, Nairobi: MIAS, p. 39; A. Pieris, 1991, *El rostro asiático de Cristo*, Salamanca: Sígueme; J. Severino Croato, 'The Hope of Immortality in the Great Cosmovisions of the East', in *Concilium* 60 (1970), pp. 19–33.

On Dying Hard: Lessons from Popular Crucifixions and Undisciplined Resurrections in Latin America

MARCELLA MARIA ALTHAUS-REID

'The cross is a symbol of redemption and life. Therefore, it cannot be presented as a form of popular protest . . . the crucifixion of people is ethically and religiously questionable.'
Document from the Roman Catholic Paraguayan Episcopal Conference, 2004.

'Los de abajo han decidido a escucharse a sí mismos.'
('Those at the bottom have decided to listen to themselves')
Colectivo La Tribu[1]

Let me start these reflections with a scene from what we could call 'the *Other* Gospel', that is, a scene from the life, crucifixion, and resurrection of people and their ideas of economic justice and peace in the midst of the current chaotic crisis of the expansion of capitalism in Latin America. The text I am going to reflect on comes from an article that appeared in an Argentine newspaper.[2] It is a scene of crucifixion. It starts by describing a group of fifteen half-starved women, some accompanied by their children, kneeling at the foot of a cross. Their almost violent crying, it is said, could be heard at some distance. Together they begged for the life of a young man, still in his early thirties, who was going to be crucified. Apparently, according to journalists, the man asked them to let it be: justice and love should, after all, prevail on this earth. What was the crucifixion of a man, he argued, when whole communities can no longer afford the minimum required for a life with dignity? Finally, the police were called to intervene and the crucified people were taken to jail, to appear before a judge called, paradoxically, Mr Centurion.

Is that scene, just described, familiar to Christian readers? It is indeed and the newspaper article can be read almost as a scene from the Gospels, except that it comes from the Paraguay of two years ago, when a group of people protested against job losses and the State's disregard for the life of the patients in a local hospital trapped by poverty. I should like to argue that this text reflects an almost canonical experience of life at the margins in a globalized economy. As the text of economic suffering and deprivation is mixed with compassion and religious undertones, one senses that a new chapter of the *Other* Gospel has become been re-inscribed. If theology (and hermeneutics) is contextual, popular crucifixions are the supplement of the Gospel in the twenty-first century in Latin America. Indeed a hermeneutics of vicarious crucifixion and sacrificial acts amidst the silence of God and the divine gestures of solidarity of the poor seem to organize the popular text of crucifixions of the excluded. The mystery and horror of the crucifixion does not diminish, but the Golgotha or site of death and despair is much closer to us.[3]

The context of this reading of the *Other* Gospel is as follows. A group of women started a hunger strike, demanding that the hospital would not cut any more jobs and resources in patient care. Suddenly, a male worker, exasperated by the lack of response to their claims, decided to be voluntarily crucified. The women tried in vain to stop him. To add to the almost surrealist scene, a doctor in the hospital also offered himself to be crucified. There would be two crosses, where two men would bleed for days, not on the outskirts of Jerusalem under a Roman army of occupation but in Paraguay under the expansion of global capitalism. Crucifixions are back, this time as the ultimate form of popular protest, extended through the masses of unemployed and impoverished people of the continent. It could be argued that crucifixions, as a form of popular protest in Latin America, reflect the fact of the more subtle but not less dramatic exemplary deaths produced by the expansion of neo-liberalism. In that sense, Jon Sobrino's well-known metaphor for El Salvador ('the crucified people') has become perversely real. Crucifixions were started by indigenous people fighting for their right, but the practice has been expanding. From bus drivers to hospital workers, people who have lost all hope have decided quite literally, to take up their crosses. For instance, statistics show that as early as in 1999 more than 8 per cent of all acts of protest in the city of Quito, Ecuador, were public voluntary crucifixions and *sangrados* (bloodletting practices).[4] As the blood of the just, clamouring to God, becomes a tangible reality, the idea of crucifixion loosed from piety suddenly appears; a dark symbol and certainly not for faint-hearted Christians.

I. The Church and Popular Crucifixions

Popular crucifixions and other bloodletting practices, such as skin cuttings in order to write protest cards with blood or the sewing of lips during hunger strikes, fill us with horror while defying any immediate theological response. As people are crucified with six-inch nails on to their crosses for days, many suffer dangerous infections which in some cases leave them disabled. As might be expected, the Roman Catholic Church in Paraguay promptly reacted to the events by strongly condemning these actions. Therefore, during the time of the crucifixions in the hospital, the Paraguayan Episcopal Conference produced a document proclaiming the sacredness of the human body while denouncing voluntary torture as sinful. The cross, as the church document says, is a symbol of life, not of popular protest.[5] Or is it? How do the excluded in Latin America understand Jesus crucified, after forty years of popular art depicting Christ as a *compañero* in solidarity and struggle against the systematic destruction of life on the continent?

The point is that beyond the complex debate on the dynamics of the voluntary and the involuntary in the crucifixion of Christ, that is, the vicarious sacrifice versus the coherent death of a religious warrior, there is more to crucifixion than mere death. In the Christian paradigm, Christ's crucifixion functions, hermeneutically speaking, as the key part of a dialectic comprising polysemic signs devised to make everyday life, and not necessarily death, meaningful. Therefore from this perspective the resurrection narrative becomes the higher point of the theology of the struggle for life, in the same way that the Latin American literary genre of Magical Realism may play a considerable part in the 'text' of crucifixions as popular protests.

Following the principle of hermeneutical suspicion in liberation theology, we can argue that our understanding of life (as of resurrection) is in fact dependent on a hermeneutics of crucifixion. Paraphrasing J. Severino Croatto, we could say, 'Tell me your understanding of the cross, and I'll tell you your idea of resurrection.'[6] Sadly, there has been a taming and disciplining of resurrection in liberation theology that is closely related to the domestication of the metaphor. Metaphors do not come from outer space, not even from sacred spaces. They come from our historical and cultural experiences of life. The problem is that we tend to forget that the cross and resurrection of Christ are metaphors referring us to a similitude not always necessarily applicable. Making sense of the cross and the resurrection of Christ lies in the community of readers, not just following a tradition but in their ability to introduce a sense of disorder or 'revelation' into the reading.

Crucifixions need to recover their novelty in life: they are going to be rethought in the alternative way of the proclaimed kingdom of God. If crucifixions regain their novelty and transgression, then the resurrection will have the possibility of announcing new life. Sadly, the resurrection narrative in the Gospels has been reified. Rather than as historical events, the cross and resurrection need to be thought of as conceptual orders, orders that can be part of a continued tradition of a community of interpreters only by opening space for new revelations. New departures need new closures. Curiously, the liberation or effective praxis of a theology of resurrection depends on a dynamic of new crucifixions.

The popular performers of crucifixions in Latin America undertake much more than social protest. The fact that they disturb us profoundly is a sign of the disruption they are introducing into the tamed meaning of the cross. The undisciplined imagination of the poor produces unpredictable theologies that help us to realize that any hermeneutics of the events of the passion of Christ today is neither self-evident nor stabilized.

What happens is that there is a hermeneutical function in the popular crucifixions of the excluded and marginalized in Latin America, which help us not just to re-read the event of Christ's death and resurrection but to reorganize a tentative hermeneutics of liberation for the twenty-first century on issues of the struggle for life and the changes in political and religious paradigms.

Facing the scene of popular crucifixions in Latin America confronts us with more than a theology of cross and resurrection, rather with a hermeneutical circle of revelations. In theology, even in liberation theology, there are no easy triumphs or theological responses to match every situation. In reading the texts of popular protests we may become aware that there are different kinds of death still hidden in the theology of crucifixion, just as there are suppressed lives claiming a resurrection. This is an important starting point that a political theology needs to consider seriously. However, a resurrection from the margins (or *of* the margins) cannot be a mere adoption of that elite theological understanding that works by producing parallel universes of understanding. The hermeneutics of relationships advocated by Clodovis Boff when he was a postgraduate student requires to be read in the critical context he intended (Boff 1980). Globalization is not the Roman Empire, neither are the crucified doctors of the hospital in Paraguay Christ. Yet, there are important hermeneutical clues to be considered in their representations and the act of empowerment that allowed them to take charge of the passion aesthetics of the Gospels.

Let us now go on to analyze the popular crucifixions in more depth, in order to re-configure (and de-objectify) at least a meaning of the resurrection amongst the poor in Latin American today. What we have here is everyday scenes of crucifixion as texts. As such, they can be read or heard in the media or seen in the news or photographs. We can even be personal witnesses and stand, literally, at the foot of the crosses. That image in itself is a text to be interpreted. However, we also have another dimension to the scenes of crucifixion: they are already theologized texts, that is, there is already a community of interpreters who through a process of cultural intertextuality have fixed some meaning into the reading. In that sense, the hermeneutics of the scenes is a biblical one, for the scriptures are also theologized experiences of life. What differentiates them are the metaphorical universes implied in the two texts from the Gospels and from the *Other* Gospel. Leaving aside the traditions and meaning of the cross amongst different Latin American nations, the fact is that Latin American Christianity does not have an imaginary conception of resurrection. In other words, there is no liberation theology of resurrection in Latin America and even less of popular resurrections. That in itself is an important clue that opens horizons of an understanding of resurrection from the reading of the gospel from the excluded in Latin America in the twenty-first century.

II. Reflections on the Crucified People

The Latin American cultural inter-text from which the Bible (or the cross, in this case) is read is made, contrary to the belief of the liberationists, not from an experience of exodus but from an experience of Canaan. At least we can say that if the intentionality of exodus existed in the Latin American imagination it was an exodus without gods. Moreover, to extend the religious image, we could say that it was an exodus where gods died or agonized with their people. People from the Original Nations had no answer to the genocide suffered, but neither had their gods. Although the cross has been considered part of an ideological indoctrination of submission used against the Original Nations,[7] more could be made of the attachment to a theology of the cross without resurrection among the Latin American people. Crucifixion could be inter-textually read as the original existential experience of the continent: that is, the sense of the sacred perished or at least was heavily devaluated and demonized for centuries to come. When José Maria Arguedas wrote in his novel *Los ríos profundos* (1987) about the ceremonies of the cross amongst indigenous people in Peru, he disclosed not only their sense of ideological alienation but also a deep identification with the experience of the cross. During Easter (*pascuas*, lit. Passover, in Spanish) the indigenous people bring a large wooden cross to the city central park and spend the whole month sitting every night beside it, crying. In Peruvian culture the entire natural world is sacred: for instance, the mountains 'get married' and have families, while animals and rivers have personality. In such a culture mourning the cross must have much more than an element of ideological alienation. The cross may be seen as a site of another type of mourning – the place where their sacred experience lost its meaning or experienced a *Pachacuti*.[8] The primordial disorder of the Peruvian universe coincides with and is allowed to express itself in the disorder of the cross.

If the Original Nations read the events of Passion Week from the perspective of their own experience of crucifixions it is because Latin America is in many ways Canaan. However, Canaan is here more than a geographical site or a metaphor for genocide. It is true that the burned lands, the sweat of the slave bodies working under duress, and the demonization of collective memories can be read from the struggle for the privatization of water and gas resources. Even at this point in the twenty-first century there is a distinctive religious imperial discourse sacralizing the motivation of the powerful nations' military expansion and struggle for hegemonic political control. However, the crucifixions of the excluded, the poorest of the poor or the *Other*, confront us as one of the most powerful ghosts of Christian faith: the crucified Canaanites. It is from them that we need to learn a resurrection theology.

III. Jesus/Canaan

The point is that the event of Canaan and the historical destruction of the Canaanites in the Bible needs to be understood as more than a metaphor or a theological verb. We already know that the event of the destruction of Canaan is a performative act in colonial Christianity that has been responsible for the dynamics and mobilization of theologized identities. However, Canaan as a term represents a dynamic of loss, mourning, and the force of theological re-inscription. Canaan is the name of the movement of re-inscription of the divine under duress, *ex-nihilo*, and against its will. In Canaan, the three paradoxes of hermeneutics – (1) memory; (2) sense of others and (3) belonging to a community (Valdés 1998) – are threatened. In what way?

First, the narrative memory of the community risks becoming fragmented by the disruption of the possibilities of tradition. Yet, Canaan is more than a term of victimization that also gives meaning to Christianity. Curiously, resurrection is more a Canaanite than an Israelite religious theme. Canaan is an event of surrogate gods and as such, the dark origin of godly sacrifices and vicariousness. The dynamics of Canaan that nurtured Latin America brought about a different aesthetics produced by a collective memory of the cross. That is, the narrativized memory of at least some sections of Latin America is interlinked with crucifixions. A deep sense of identity with Christ may mean that people have seen themselves in the metaphor of dying gods.

Second, in the sense that we need others to define our identity, the cross as the ultimate example of the meaning of being an *Other* also becomes a form of communication; that is, it conveys a collective identity in dialogue. This is why the images of workers crucifying themselves or cutting their arms to use their blood to write notes of protest to the government fill us with deep horror. It is just this that the Roman Catholic Church in Paraguay condemns. The popular crucifixions as protest inauguration seem to violate something pre-established in the linguistic community of the Church, a community used to a sense of the proper use of authority based on logocentrism. The disruption of communication comes now from the self-mutilation of bodies. This time it is voluntary, but such was not the case during the years of military dictatorship, when the mutilation was not always condemned by the Church. It seems as if the voluntary aspect (linked to a sense of empowerment) is the disruptive and scandalous action. The re-inscription of the cross in the midst of the protest against globalization re-actualizes the perverted edges of the cross that theology has been practising for centuries. Now, amongst the crucified protesters of Latin America, the cross becomes not a contrast but justice itself because of the irregularity of these crosses (and possible resurrections). We are in the presence of a non-linear type of resurrection event: the popular crucifixions represent a breakthrough into a possible theology of resurrection from the dispossessed. This time, the event is not the resurrection of Christ but the resurrection of Canaan itself. Jesus himself has become the ultimate Canaanite, but the resurrection of Canaan is also a verb: it announces dynamics and gestures previously unknown. The excluded are assuming those of God in themselves. As the podcast of the Argentinian collective *La Tribu* says, '*los de abajo han decidido a escucharse a sí mismos*' (those at the bottom have decided to listen to themselves).

I said at the beginning of this article that there is no possibility anymore of writing triumphal theologies, not even amongst liberationists. The popular crucifixions are hermeneutically opaque narratives, where metaphors and configurations have been profoundly altered. Many years ago, when Jürgen Moltmann, in his *Theology of Hope*, spoke of the resurrection, he claimed that death was never to be again a frontier but a site of revelation. Yet here we are seeing the contrary: death (as deadly structures amongst us, such as imperial and neo-liberal policies) needs to become again a frontier or we shall lose the power to act. Why? Because frontiers can be re-inscribed and deconstructed, and this is what popular crucifixions in a way are doing. Without death as a frontier we are in the domain of absolutes. Somehow, the revelations in popular crucifixions show us the need to find a theological praxis of resurrection, instead of an approved chapter of the reification of the theologised meaning of death, and alternative ways of collective life.

In the particular setting of twenty-first-century Latin America, the military authoritarianism of the twentieth century seems far away, but neo-liberalism has destroyed the democratic system of relationships as the State disintegrates. It is not only the State that has left a vacuum in the mediation of processes of social justice; other symbolic spaces of the poor, such as the rural schools, have collapsed. During the military regimes the Church produced alternative sources of Christian mediations such as the basic communities and parish networks. Curiously, the Christian mediations succeeded in supporting the identity and agency of citizenship as an element for social change. However, neo-liberalism may already have disrupted the location of churches as centres for citizen networks. It could be that popular crucifixions are telling us that Canaan dies hard, and that therein also lies our hope. It is the possibility of disordering theology by the poor, destabilizing heroes and paradigms, that in an opaque way is signalling the end of a theological era and the beginning of another, where the Christian memory of the mystery of the cross and resurrection will be built around the present context of despair and defiance.

Bibliography
Arguedas, José Maria (1987), *Los ríos profundos*. Madrid: Alianza.
Boff, Clodovis (1980), *Teología de lo político. Sus mediaciones*. Salamanca: Sígueme.
Valdés, Mario J. (1998), *Hermeneutics of Poetic Sense. Critical Studies of Literature, Cinema and Cultural History*. Toronto: University of Toronto Press.

Notes

1. *La Tribu* is an alternative radio station from Buenos Aires, Argentina. Its address is La Tribu 88.7 FM (www.podcast.fmlatribu.com).
2. This text comes from Marta Dillon's article 'Simplemente sangre' in *Página* 12, 27 June 2004. The protest actions were taken against the Instituto de Previsión Social de Paraguay (IPS).
3. For a reflection on the violence of the economic paradigm of the cross as a redemptive event (thus linked to an economy of debt) see my chapter 'Lunch-Time Crucifixions' in R. Radford Ruether and L. Isherwood (eds), 2007, *Weep not for your Children. Essays on Religion and Violence* (London: Equinox).
4. Cf. the article by uis Angel Saavedra from the Fundación Regional de Asesoría en Derechos Humanos, 'Medidas de Hecho y Control Social en el Ecuador durante 1999.' Available on line, Http://derechos.org/inredh/doc/medidas.html.
5. The complete document from the Church can be found in Http://episcopal.org.py/comunicados/oladecrucifixiones.html.
6. Croatto used to say to his students in Buenos Aires 'Tell me your hermeneutical methodology and I'll tell you your exegesis on any given text.'
7. The use of the cross as submission and the fact that the church practically ignored resurrection has been studied by several Latin American authors, notably by Juan Mackay in his pioneer book, 1950, *El Otro Cristo Español* (Mexico City: CUPSA).
8. *Pachacuti* or *Pachakutiq* in Quechua means literally 'world-turner.' The Incas used the term to express their understanding that with the arrival of the European invaders, the world became chaotic and unintelligible, that is, upside down.

II. The Specifically Christian Vision

Resurrection in the Israelite Tradition

SENÉN VIDAL

The divergencies in research into interpretation of Old Testament and ancient Judaic evidence on resurrection are really surprising.[1] This is clearly due to the lack of clarity in the texts themselves, which contain a broad variety of representations, some of them mutually contradictory. To delineate a coherent, let alone genealogical, sequence of them appears to be a very difficult, if not impossible, task. Despite this, I think one major cause of the confusion is the lack of precision in the *scenario* or general framework into which the different texts can be fitted. The present article focuses its attention on this scenario, hoping in this way to make a small contribution within the structure established by the editors of this issue of *Concilium*.[2]

I. Communion with the dead

(a) The scenario of the Israelite tradition was based on an anthropological and cosmological view that the people of Israel shared to a large extent with the ancient peoples surrounding them, according to which the whole of reality is founded on a *mysterious communion*.[3] Communion in the integral life of a person, without the dichotomy of separate spheres; communion of individuals with the social group – family, clan, tribe, nation – in whose bosom their whole life unfolded, in a mutual flux and reflux of life; communion of the human group with its ecological environment, in deep interconnectedness and interdependence. And the whole of this complex communion was continually sustained by the mystery of God's communion with his creation. Because the sovereign God's creative working of 'justice' (*sedeq*) lies at the base of all reality, founding, keeping, and restoring the creational and salvational order in which the life of the human community in its multiple manifestations can flourish and bear fruit, and extending even to its relations with the animal world and with the land it cultivates and inhabits. Human existence thereby acquires an eminently dynamic and relational character.

This general framework is, in my view, decisive for the question of the *destiny of the dead* in the Israelite tradition. Our greatest difficulty in understanding this perhaps derives from our own view of human reality. This is fairly far removed from the Israelite one, in that, in contrast to that, our view tends to be entitative and disintegrative, separating the various manifestations of human life into disparate elements, and basically individualist in nature, with its focus of attention on individuals on their own and in their own particular destiny.

(b) The Israelite religious outlook was clearly focused on God's faithfulness to the alliance with his chosen *people in history*. It was precisely in the unfolding of the history of this people, with all its changing circumstances, that the presence and liberating action of this God was to be found. It is, then, natural for the Israelite religious experience to focus its interest on the real historical world of the living and not on the world of the dead, since it was effectively the living, and not the dead, who were the agents of the historical journey of the people. This realist and historically embodied disposition is something that is very plain in the oldest Israelite tradition, and it remained like this, overall, throughout its later development. But this did not exclude but rather included a mysterious *communion of the dead* with the people of the living. The latter, not the former, were indeed the focal point of this communion. The dead were mysteriously bound up with the destiny of the historical people of the living, through their descendants and the actions they had carried out in their lifetime. They stayed in communion even with the land in which they had lived, since this was the land of the historical journey of the people (see Gen. 23).

Death as the conclusion of a full life was seen as completely integrated, with no friction, into this scenario, since it accorded with the order of creation established by God. On the other hand, though, premature death, which implied a failed life, suggested divine punishment. The *problem* arose in the cases of premature death without apparent justification. A voice of protest against this type of death can be found in the *resurrections* of the prematurely dead recounted in the Israelite tradition of the prophetic figures of Elijah (1 Kgs 17.17–24) and Elisha (2 Kgs 4.18–37; 13.20–21). In these cases, we are dealing with newly dead persons being returned to life, through a sort of special healing, and not yet of the resurrection of the dead and their definitive transformation into fullness of life at the time of the people's final liberation. But they are already indicative of faith in the power of the Lord of life and death, in whose name the prophetic figures act, and also of rebellion against the destructive potential of death, both key motives that later mould hope in the resurrection and the definitive transformation of the dead.

(c) The decisive element of the Israelite scenario was *communion with God*, as this underpinned communion within the people and within creation. If God were truly the Lord of the living and the dead, this communion with God had to overcome the barrier of death itself. This basic tenet of Israelite religious outlook matured into two types of representations concerning the destiny of the *righteous* at the end of their lives.

(1) The first representation was *ascension* to the realm of God without experiencing death. Early Israelite tradition reserved this category to two special figures; the patriarch Enoch (Gen. 5.24) and the prophet Elijah (2 Kgs 2.1–18). But later Judaic tradition amplified it and applied it to other personages: Melchisedech, Moses, Pinchas, Baruch, Esdras.[4] One very significant feature of this representation needs signalling out: far from distancing these individuals from communion with the historical people, the effect of their special destiny of communion with God was to assure their special link with the ultimate liberation of this people. These figures ascended to the realm of God were, in the tradition, to play a special role in the destiny of the people, as revealers and agents of the salvific events of the end time.

(2) Nevertheless, the commonest representation of the fate of the righteous was the affirmation of the permanence of their communion with God *after their death*. Actual specifications of this varied considerably. But what kindled this hope was probably the experience of *oppression and violence* undergone by the righteous. It then became a matter of the consequence of trust in God's faithfulness or liberating justice toward his oppressed faithful. This is, specifically, the hope expressed in veiled terms in certain texts in which the clamour of the persecuted just is heard (Pss 49.15–16; 73.23–8). Later, it is expressed in full clarity in Wisdom 3.1–10 and numerous Judaic texts.[5]

Just as with the first representation, so in this type the communion of the righteous dead with God establishes their communion with the destiny of the *historical people*, since it guarantees their sharing in the final liberation of the people. This is sometimes indicated by expressly pointing out that these righteous dead will share in the future resurrection, though at other times this aspect does not appear explicitly. This is the case with the much-debated text of Wisdom 3.1–10, in which the present communion of the righteous dead with God (vv. 1–6) will lead to their future splendid triumph over their oppressors in the time of the ultimate manifestation of the reign of God (vv. 7–10).[6] In this sense, we can talk of an 'intermediate state' of the dead, waiting for their final fullness. Despite the somewhat confused *mises en scène* of some texts, however, I do think that their perspective is not the anthropological one of the imperfect state of the dead, or that of the imperfection of their communion with God, but precisely that of their communion in the future liberation of the people in history. In this sense, it can certainly be said that the situation of the dead will find its fulfilment in final salvation of the whole people.

(d) All things considered, it is not surprising that this final representation of the communion of the righteous dead with God should, in certain texts of *Hellenist Judaism*, have the anthropological dualism typical of Hellenism applied to it. This results in their speaking of the immortal soul, freed in death from the prison of the body so as to enter into full communion with God. Significant representatives of this tendency are Philo of Alexandria and 4 Maccabees, a text that gives this interpretation to the notion of the resurrection of the martyrs of the Maccabean rebellion described in 2 Maccabees. Certain writings of Flavius Josephus, trying to explain the Israelite tradition in Hellenic language, also tend in this direction.[7] These Judaic documents are certainly very significant, in that they bear witness to a conjunction of the typical Israelite tradition with the Hellenic. There is, however, no getting away from the individualist, other-worldly, and a-historical bent of the Hellenic dualist conception, which is pretty far removed from the scenario of the Israelite tradition set out above.[8]

Hope of resurrection

(a) The horizon of hope in the Israelite scenario was the ultimate renewal of the *history* of the Israelite people in a transformed land and, through this, the renewal of the history of all the other peoples on earth. This was the permanent horizon of Israel's hope. It was frequently expressed in the powerful symbol of the reign or *sovereignty of God*, the future definitive manifestation of which it constantly hoped for from the period of the Exile, normally in connection with hope in the messianic age.[9] The character of this symbol, which Jesus took up as the focus of his proclamation and actions, was essentially creational and historical.[10] In it, Israel was expressing its hope in the final implementation of God's liberating justice, which would transform the calamitous state of the people through liberation from every type of slavery

and oppression, and the outcome of which would be enjoyment of a state of total peace and fullness of life. This would be the moment when God's sovereignty over this history and this earth was finally displayed. This means that Israel did not – in any way – expect another world, beyond history and transcendent, but only the transformation of the state of this historical one, beginning with the renovation of the people of Israel and ending in the renovation of all the peoples of the world. This is the tone of the whole of the Old Testament and of the literature of ancient Judaism, whose thoroughly materialistic and naturalistic images do not in any way indicate a spiritual world but only this historical and earthly one. The ultimate basis for this has to be found in faith in the creator and liberator God, indefectibly faithful to his creation and his people.

In connection with this, it is worth pointing out, in the light of extensive interpretation, that the hope of the *apocalyptic current* had this same creational and historical character, so that what apocalyptic brought was not a new hope, but a radical new disposition of traditional Israelite hope.[11] Faith in the creator God and in historical liberation also underpinned apocalyptic hope. The function of the apocalyptic vision was to re-animate the ancestral hope in a crisis situation, unveiling the great seriousness of the historical moment and steeling people to face it with courage. In this way the apocalyptic vision represented a vigorous attempt at active response in the face of the experience of extreme alienation and oppression, summoning the people to endurance and commitment in the struggle, with their hope set on the great transformation that was drawing near.

(b) This horizon provides the setting for hope in the *resurrection* of the dead, a theme developed in apocalyptic, though not exclusive to it or originating in it. What this theme suggests is precisely the renewal of the complete historical existence of the people, within a renewed creation (cf. Is. 11.6–9; 32.15–20; 35.1–10; 65.17–25; 66.2). This *outlook* is well expressed in the texts where the theme of resurrection of the dead is used precisely as a powerful *image* for the restoration of the nation destroyed, in a state of 'death'.[12] The wider development of the image is found in the impressive prophetic vision of Ezekiel 37.1–14, which shows the renewal of the 'dead' exiled nation as an authentic new creation by means of the spirit of life of the creator God. The image appears again in a similar sense in Hosea 6.1–3 (and 13.14), in reference to the revival of a people devastated by foreign oppression. And perhaps Isaiah 52.13 – 53.12 is referring to the same context as Ezekiel 37 when it speaks of the restoration of the Servant of Yahweh,

representing Israel in the situation of exile, after having been stricken to the point of death.[13] The image of resurrection employed in these texts describes, with unusual vividness, the future renovation of the people as a genuine new creation brought about by the God of life. This clearly implies a profound transformation of the historical course of the nation in all aspects of its life.

(c) This final renewal of the history of the people is the framework for the *real* resurrection of the dead members of that people. Resurrection here has the function of doing justice to the faithful fallen through their faithfulness to God, so that they can take part in the definitive liberation of the whole people. Its context, then, is not the anthropological one of individuals but the communal one of making the people new as a whole, in which individuals are included as members. Resurrection is not understood without this *community* dimension, since the existence of the risen, just like the present life of the living, is immersed in a mystery of communion, founded in communion with the creator and liberator God. And this implies that resurrection has to include a *renewal* of one's complete human existence as creature of the creator God, with all one's history, with all one has lived with hands and heart and in communion with one's human group and with the creation in which one's existence has been set. Resurrection, then, cannot fall into the reductionism of an individual type of anthropological representation, entitative and static, as happens so often, but needs always to preserve the global and dynamic perspective of the integral re-awakening of human existence, in its entire historical and creaturely dimension.

The clearest witnesses to resurrection are those referring to the situation of resistance to the *Hellenizing* agenda of Antioch IV. Daniel 12.1–3 (and 12.13) belong to this context, speaking of the resurrection and glorious transformation of the fallen faithful, in contrast to the ignominious destiny of those who oppose them, so they can thereby share in the salvation of their people, when the longed-for kingdom of God takes shape in the people, eliminating the oppressing foreign dominions (see Dan. 2 and 7).[14] Later, 2 Maccabees (7.14, 37–46; 12.38–46) refers to this same context when it speaks of the resurrection of those who died in the Maccabean resistance by the creator and liberator God.[15]

This type of hope of resurrection is *the oldest* within the Israelite tradition. It is most likely already attested in the special section of Isaiah 24 – 27, which should be dated back to the Persian period, perhaps to a situation of persecution within that.[16] In this context, very similar to that of Daniel and 2

Maccabees, the hope is proclaimed that the God of righteousness will raise the faithful martyred in the persecution (Is. 26.19; 25.8), so that they can share in the liberation of the humiliated people, when the glorious reign of God over his people will be manifest (Is. 24.23). This same hope for the resurrection of the faithful oppressed also features in old parts of 1 Enoch (22 – 27; 91 – 105), some of which are earlier than Daniel.[17]

(d) The theme of *resurrection* was greatly developed in *later Israelite tradition*.[18] It is amply attested in apocalyptic literature (as in the Parables of 1 Enoch 37 – 71, the Life of Adam and Eve, 4 Esdras, 2 Baruch), in extra-apocalyptic (such as the Psalms of Solomon, Biblical Antiquities, Testaments of the Patriarchs), in the writings deriving from the Qumran community (such as 4Q 521, 4Q 385, 1QH 14),[19] in liturgical texts (second blessing in the Shemone Esre prayer), and in rabbinic literature. An important strand in this development, also taken up by early Christianity, was giving a resurrection interpretation to numerous scriptural texts that did not originally have this meaning. It was natural, then, that this type of interpretation should have a decisive influence on Greek translations of scripture, beginning with the old one of the LXX, and on Aramaic ones (targumim).

Two significant aspects of this development of tradition should be mentioned. The first refers to varied speculation on the *time*, *place*, and *means* of the resurrection event. On the theme of means especially, there appear the strangest and most varied representations and stagings, which have nothing to do with the sobriety of the ancient tradition. The speculation in many of them, focused on a crude mechanics of the human organism, certainly does not reflect the deep meaning of resurrection as a new creation by the God of life. The second aspect is the *generalization* of resurrection to the whole of humankind, so as to guarantee God's universal judgment. As a result, two types of resurrection are distinguished: one to salvation and another to condemnation. And this implies two types of transformation for the risen: one of glory and one of ignominy. This has the effect of specifying God's justice in a universal dimension, but at the same time the essentially liberating tone of resurrection and transformation that marked the ancient tradition becomes somewhat diluted.

(e) To sum up the above exposition, I believe that a good *compendium* of the meaning of Israelite hope in the resurrection of the dead is provided in the traditional Judaic formula Paul cites in Romans 4.17, to define the faith of Abraham, father of all believers in the God who has brought in the messianic

era.[20] The liberating action of the God 'who gives life to the dead' is the ultimate manifestation of the creator God, of the One who 'calls into existence the things that do not exist'. In this way, the creator God is shown to be the God who remains faithful to his creation to the end. Resurrection thus becomes the definitive new creation, which unveils the deepest sense of the kingdom of God over his creation, by converting the God of truth into the One who is 'all in all' (1 Cor. 15.28).

Translated by Paul Burns

Notes

1. The most significant study among recent research is É. Puech, 1993, *La croyance des esséniens en la vie future: Immortalité, résurrection, vie éternelle? Histoire d'une croyance dans le judaïsme ancien, I: La résurrection des morts et le contexte scriptuaire, II: Les données qumraniennes et classiques*, EtB 21–22, Paris. Besides a detailed analysis of the texts and archaeological data from Qumran and of the ancient witnesses to the Essenes (vol. II), he presents a good overview of investigation into the texts of the Old Testament, of Judaism, and of early Christianity (vol. I). Among other recent studies, I single out M. É. Boismard, 1995, *Faut-il encore parler de 'résurrection'?*, Paris: Cerf; A. Chester, 'Resurrection and transformation', in F. Avemarie and H. Lichtenberger (eds), 2001, *Auferstehung – Resurrection* (WUNT 135), Tübingen, pp. 47–77); J. Collins, 1993, *Daniel. A Commentary on the Book of Daniel*, Minneapolis: Fortress Press, pp. 390-98; J. Day, 'The Development of Belief in Life after Death in Ancient Israel', in J. Barton and D. Reimer (eds), 1996, *After the Exile. Essays in Honor of Rex Mason*, Macon: Mercer Univ. Press, pp. 231–57; A. A. Fischer, *Tod und Jenseits im Alten Orient und im Alten Testament*. Neukirch/Vluyn: Neukirchener; Ch. Grappe, 'Naissance de l'idée de la résurrection dans le judaïsme', in O. Mainville and D. Marguerat (eds), 2001, *Résurrection. L'après-mort dans le monde ancien et le Nouveau Testament*, Geneva/Montreal: Labor et Fides/Médiaspaul, pp. 45–72; E. Haag, 2003, *Das hellenisischer Zeitalter. Israel und das Bibel im 4. bis 1. Jahrhundert v. Chr.* (Biblische Enzyklopädie 9), Stuttgart: Kohlhammer, pp. 245–52; M. Hengel, 'Das Begräbnis Jesu bei Paulus und die liebliche Auferstehung aus dem Grabe', in Avemarie and Lichtenberger, *op. cit.*, pp. 119–83 (here 150–72); B. Janowski, 'Die Toten Loben JHWH nicht. Psalm 88 und das alttestamentliche Todesverständis', in, 2003, *Der Gott des Lebens. Beiträge zur Theologie des Alten Testaments 3*, Neukirche/Vluyn: Neukirchener, pp. 201–43; H. Lichtenberger, 'Resurrection in the Intertestamental Literature and Rabbinic Theology', in *Concilium* 1993/5, pp. 23–31; É. Puech, 'Mesianismo, escatología y resurrección en los manuscritos del Mar Muerto', in J. Trebolle Barrera (ed.), 1999, *Paganos, judíos y cristianos en los textos de*

Qumrán, Madrid: Trotta, pp. 245–86; N. T. Wright, 2003, *The Resurrection of the Son of God. Christian Origins and the Question of God*, III, Minneapolis: Fortress Press, pp. 85–206.
2. It is important to note that the scenario of resurrection in the tradition of Jesus and of early Christianity continued and developed that of the Israelite tradition: see S. Vidal, 2003, *Los tres proyectos de Jesús y el cristianismo naciente. Un ensayo de reconstrucción histórica*, Salamanca: Sígueme, pp. 187, 259–60, 273–6, 290–304; idem., 2005, *El proyecto mesiánico de Pablo*, Salamanca: Sígueme, pp. 215–34.
3. S. Vidal, *Proyectos*, pp. 65–6; *Mesiánico*, pp. 80–4; also the good studies by B. Janowski in *Der Gott des Lebens, op. cit.*, pp. 75–133, 157–95.
4. Texts in Ch. Grappe, 'Naissance', pp. 63–9.
5. A. A. Fischer, *Tod*, pp. 158–65; Ch. Grappe, 'Naissance', pp. 63–9; B. Janowski, 'Toten', pp. 35–45; N. T. Wright, *Resurrection*, pp. 103–8.
6. É. Puech, *Croyance, I*, pp. 92–8; Wright, *Resurrection*, pp. 162–75.
7. M. Hengel, 'Begräbnis', pp. 161–5; Wright, *Resurrection*, pp. 140–6, 175–81.
8. On this point A. Torres Queiruga makes interesting observations in, 2003, *Repensar la resurrección. La diferencia cristiana en la continuidad de las religiones y la cultura*, Madrid: Trotta, pp. 138–143.
9. S. Vidal, *Proyectos*, pp, 38–45.
10. *Ibid.*, p. 139–75; idem, 2006, *Jesús el Galileo*, Santander: Sal Terrae, pp. 107–40.
11. *Proyectos*, pp. 55–60.
12. Cf. especially A. Chester, 'Resurrection', pp. 47–59.
13. R. Albertz, 2001, *Die Exilszeit. 6. Jahrhundert v. Chr* (Biblische Enzyklopädie 7), Stuttgart: Kohlhammer, pp. 317–19.
14. Chester, 'Resurrection', pp. 59–64; Haag, 'Zeitalter', pp. 248–50; Puech, *Croyance I*, pp. 79–85; Wright, *Resurrection*, pp. 109–15.
15. Hengel, 'Begräbnis', pp. 159–61; Puech, *Croyance I*, pp. 85–92; Wright, *Resurrection*, pp. 150–3.
16. H. D. Preuss, 1999, *Teología del Antiguo Testamento II. El camino de Israel con Yahvé*, Bilbao: DDB, p. 258.
17. Puech, *Croyance I*, pp. 105–16; Wright, *Resurrection*, pp. 154–7.
18. For an analysis of this very widespread tradition see P. Billerbeck, [6]1975, *Kommentar zum Neuen Testaments aus Talmud und Midrasch IV/2*, Munich, pp. 1166–98; Grappe, 'Naissance', pp. 50–60; Hengel, 'Begräbnis', pp. 150–72; Puech, *Croyance I*, pp. 99–242, and II; Wright, *Resurrection*, pp. 129–206.
19. This is the outcome of the basic study by Puech, *Croyance II*.
20. Analysis of the formula in Vidal, 1982, *La resurrección de Jesús en las cartas de Pablo. Analísis de las tradiciones*, Salamanca: Sígueme, pp. 17–30.
21. Idem, *Mesiánico*, pp. 232–4.

Jesus Raised as 'Primrose' of Shared Resurrection

GIUSEPPE BARBOGLIO

A non-ingenuous reading of the New Testament texts seeks to understand their metaphorical language by familiarizing ourselves with the actual metaphors: awakening from the sleep of death and raising from the earth, exalting one who descended below, ascension into heaven, appearance, empty tomb. Their function is to communicate realities and experiences that go beyond the confines of our human world and express events belonging to the divine sphere attainable only through the eyes of faith. There is no description of what happened to Jesus; this appears only with the apocryphal Gospel of Peter, from the second century (9.34ff). In truth, we are faced with the indescribable, the untellable. Kessler does not amaze us when he states: 'A video camera installed in the tomb would not have recorded anything' (1999, *La risurrezione di Gesù Cristo*, Brescia, p. 438). In the canonical writings we have the testimonies of Peter and his companions, not excluding Paul, who expound on their experiences: they have met the crucified Jesus in their lives as a functioning presence – the apparitions – and have intuited that God has raised, exalted, and glorified him. Over the centuries readers have been confronted directly with their confession of faith emerging from an experience of the risen Christ and have been able to become involved with him, distinguishing at the same time between historical resurrection experience and confessions of the risen Christ.

The central nucleus communicated by the New Testament writings is provided by the collective account of the *paschal events*, but not so much in themselves as in the lived witness of the first believers. Starting from this point, we can seize the hidden meaning. The creed of the early Church recites: 'that he was raised on the third day according to the scriptures, and that he appeared to Cephas, then to the twelve' (1 Cor. 15.4–5), or: 'The Lord has risen indeed and has appeared to Simon!' (Luke 24.34). Resurrection and apparition are the two essential paschal events: the first

Jesus Raised as 'Primrose' of Shared Resurrection

concerns Jesus, his divinizing metamorphosis, as one might say; the second indicates the experience of encounter of Peter and his companions with Christ who comes to meet them. And it is from this experience that they 'deduce' that he who was crucified has been raised to life by God.

I. The appearances

It seems opportune to start from these as attested in confessions of faith but also, in more or less colourful versions, in three Gospels (cf. Matt. 28, Luke 24, and John 20 – 21). The catastrophe of Good Friday had caused the pre-paschal faith of Peter and his companions to collapse, symbolized by their flight into Galilee (Matt. 26.56): they had gone back to the remote past, cancelling the recent past of their life shared with Jesus. But shortly after this they are confessing that God has raised the crucified Jesus, making him the first of the risen and the beginning of resurrection for the world and humankind. They have arrived at this faith because 'he has shown himself to them' (ôphthê). The Greek verb that translates the Hebrew equivalent in reflexive mode was used to indicate the theophany of God appearing to Abraham (Gen. 17.10), to Moses (Exod. 3.2), and to others. Equally, Jesus' 'appearing' does not indicate an ocular vision but rather a Christophany; he has come forth to meet Peter and companions. It is not they who 'see' him and go out to meet him; on the contrary, it is he who comes to meet them, showing himself gifted with divine power capable of transforming their hearts and their lives. What has come about is that a psychological catastrophe has given birth to a personal 'resurrection': they have risen to a new experience of trust in Jesus.

How could this have happened? They have questioned themselves, gone back over their memories of the Master's words and actions; they have, one presumes, meditated on the scriptures and concluded that this spiritual resurrection of theirs is not self-induced: it is not a psychological process of rationalization from the struggle of their loss, rather a gift of grace from Jesus himself. They interpreted this as 'appearances', his new way of relating to Peter and his companions, different from the shared life of his earthly existence and similar to that which God has with people.

The final outcome from an interpretative process that could not be more detailed was their acceptance and affirmation that he had been raised by God, becoming the Lord, the principle capable of bringing the dead to life, he who had given them life by drawing them out of desperation and bringing them to a fresh faith and a new life. In short, he has come out to meet us, they said – the Easter appearance – and so he is the risen one and, at the same time, the one who raises to life.

II. Resurrection

This is the metaphor with which Peter and his companions interpreted the extraordinary encounter they had experienced, the 'appearance' of Christ not to their eyes but to their lives. It is precisely a theological category suggested by Hebraic tradition, indicating an event that has concerned Jesus but also involves the destiny of the world and of the human race. Therefore it is not a private event, nor is it a meteor unexpectedly appearing and equally unexpectedly disappearing; it is rather an event that takes place behind one's back, so to speak, but also one that covers the present and promises the future.

For our single word 'resurrection' Greek uses two verbs (*egeirô* and *anistêmi*), which express re-awakening from sleep and raising from the earth and are used in a metaphorical sense in the New Testament witness: the crucified Jesus is awakened by God from the sleep of his death; God has raised up from the ground the deceased Jesus lying in the earth. It is with good reason that the oldest Christian texts speak of bringing Christ 'up from the dead' (*'ek ton nekron'*; Rom. 10.7; Col. 1.18). Jesus has been made to come out of the dark halls of *sheol* or from Hades or from hell. The earliest formulas point to God as the active subject of resurrection: he has raised the crucified with his creative power of life. Nailed to the cross and descended into the realm of the dead, Jesus no longer had any possibility, on his own, of coming out from it. Everything has come about through a liberating initiative by his God.

Those who used this metaphor were people of Hebraic culture. In the Greek world no one would ever have said that Jesus was raised, given what was asserted by, for example, Aeschylus: 'so resurrection does not exist' (*Eumenides* 647f), and Plotinus: 'the true re-awakening is a resurrection *from the body, not with the body*' (*Enneades* 3, 6, 70–72). This metaphor was in use in certain sectors of the Judaism of the time, as among the Pharisees, as Flavius Josephus (2.163–5) and the New Testament (Mark 12.18–27; Acts 23.6–9) testify: people hoped in the final resurrection, especially of the righteous (cf. also Dan. 12.1–2; 1 Enoch 51.1–5). But Jesus' case brought in major originalities: it is the resurrection not of all, or of all the righteous, but of one person, and it is an event that has already taken place. Furthermore, it is not a glorious martyr who has been raised, as in the case of the Maccabees

Jesus Raised as 'Primrose' of Shared Resurrection

(cf. 2 Mac. 7), but a person crucified, so one cursed by God, according to the famous saying of Deuteronomy 21, taken up by Paul in Galatians 3.13: 'Cursed is everyone who hangs on a tree'. This means that our destiny is no longer to remain forever nailed to the wood of a cross: the crucified Jesus, un-nailed by God, brings a promise to the innumerable crucified people of history.

Above all, 'Christ has been raised from the dead, the first fruits of those who have died' (1 Cor. 15.20–21), the 'primrose' among spring flowers, as the poet Giovanni Testori says. First fruits were the earliest fruits from the countryside offered in the temple as a sign of gratitude to God, who had given the earth and made its fruits germinate. By using this metaphor, Paul is stating that it is not a matter of the resurrection of an individual alone: he is the first of those locked up in the realm of the dead to be set free by God; 'those who belong to Christ' will follow. The risen Jesus is 'the firstborn from the dead' (*'prôtotokos ek tôn nekrôn'*; Col. 1.18; cf. Rev. 1.5). Paradoxical, a birth from the dark dominion of death! The first, so not the only one. The relationship is, however, not one of a simple first and later; it is rather an intrinsic link: the resurrection of Jesus involves the resurrection of others, because he is raised as the one who raises. Paul clarifies this through making use of the Adam-Christ parallelism, a cultural means of expressing the life-giving capacity of the crucified Jesus. 'For since death came through a human being, the resurrection of the dead has also come through a human being; for as all die in Adam, so all will be made alive in Christ' (1 Cor. 15.21–2). He says much the same a little further on: 'Thus it is written, "The first man, Adam, became a living being (*psychê zôsa*)"; the last Adam [that of the end time brought into the world by Christ] became a life-giving spirit (*pneuma zôopoioun*)' (1 Cor. 15.45). 'Spirit' in the Hebrew tradition means God's power of life, the one 'who gives life to the dead (*zôopoiountos tous nekrous*)' (Rom 4.17). We might say that Christ has become the concentration of the divine life-giving power: as beneficiary of liberation from the dominion of the dead through the intervention of his God, he has in his turn become the one who is capable of giving life to the dead – we might use the image of the magnetic field of the spiritual forces of the new earth. The reference is of course to his final action of giver of life, but already in the present he is 'spiritually active', active, that is, with the power of the Spirit of God.

A good synthesis of the changes undergone by the risen Jesus is expressed in the title 'Lord' (*kyrios*). In Romans 10.9 the apostle says, 'If you confess with your lips that Jesus is Lord and believe in your heart that God raised him from the dead, you will be saved'. Note the parallelism between 'confess', a faith socialized in the credal formula, and inner belief, of the heart. But the object of both confession and belief is still the same: the raised Jesus has become the Lord. His lordship does not indicate prescriptive authority but rather saving power, divine power given to him through the grace of the One who in the Hebrew scriptures was called precisely 'the Lord', *Adonai*, *Kyrios*. 'Everyone who calls on the name of the Lord shall be saved' (Rom. 10.13): this refers to Jesus everything that was referred to Adonai by the prophets.

So in the resurrection-event, witnessed by Peter and the first believers, Jesus has been transformed into a new being, a divine being. He is still the one who was crucified, but 'in another form' (Mark 16.12). 'Form' (*morphê*) is here not something external and peripheral; it touches the depths of a person, determines the essential condition of life. Jesus has gone through a process of deep change whereby he has become the Lord, the Spirit who creates life where there is death, the first who will draw all others straight to him, bringing them out of the realm of the dead. All this is summed up in the metaphor: God has raised him up / he has been raised up by God. Therefore it is not an event we can grasp with our body's eyes or through reason; it can only be confessed in the life-experience of faith, as it was by Peter and his companions.

III. Polyphony of language

We are dealing with an event witnessed in *rich and varied ways*. The metaphorical language of resurrection is not the only one, though it is the most utilized in tradition. The testimonies in the New Testament also speak of glorification, exaltation, and ascension into heaven, not only of vindication of the cause of the crucified Jesus: different usages to signify a reality so full of meaning as to require various expressions capable of bringing out its several aspects. Now a second metaphor, parallel to the first expressed by Peter and companions, is that of *lifting up*. This expresses the high-low antithetical schema. Jesus crucified has been ex-alted, that is raised high, having been laid low by the ultimate humiliation of the cross. This is sung in the (probably pre-Pauline) hymn of Philippians 2.6–11: '[He] who, though he was in the form of God (*en morphê-i theou*) . . . emptied himself, taking the form of a slave (*morphên doulou*) . . . he humbled himself and became obedient to the point of death – even death on a cross'. This maximum abasement has been answered by God's initiative: 'Therefore God also highly exalted him (*hyperypsoun*), and gave him the name that is above every name', the name of Lord. If the incarnation is descent (*katabasi*), the resurrection is *anabasi*, raising up to the divine sphere. The spatial metaphor summarizes his historical and meta-historical life-experience: he was on high and came down low, into the human world, a descent in which he touched the depths. But God has replaced him on high, not just putting him back where he was originally, but set on a still higher level, naming him and establishing him as universal Lord, of all those 'in heaven, on earth, and under the earth', as the text says (v. 10).

The same spatial metaphor recurs in the fourth Gospel: 'And just as Moses lifted up the serpent in the wilderness, so must the Son of Man be lifted up (*hypoun*)' in the glory of the cross, to the salvation of all who believe in him (3.14–15). 'No one has ascended into heaven except the one who descended from heaven (*anabebēken, ho katabas*)' (3.13). A variant of the abasement/lifting up binomial is the humiliation/glorification antithesis, present above all in John: God has honoured the crucified one by clothing him in his divine splendour (glory). So before being lifted up on the cross Jesus prayed for what John takes as the glorification of him who has been lifted up: 'So now, Father, glorify me in your own presence with the glory that I had in your presence before the world existed' (17.5).

The metaphor of ascension into heaven (*analēmpsis/analambanein*) follows the spatial pattern: 'He was . . . taken up in [divine] glory', sings the christological hymn of 1 Timothy 3.16. Luke for his part provides an account furnished with chronological and topographical data: 'Then he led them out as far as Bethany, and, lifting up his hands, he blessed them. While he was blessing them he withdrew from them and was carried up into heaven' (24.50–51). This also true of Acts 1, where the ascent into heaven of the risen Christ is connected to his last coming: 'This Jesus, who has been taken from you into heaven, will come in the same way as you saw him go into heaven' (v. 11). What this is actually describing is passing from the human sphere to the divine.

Another metaphor, now juridical in tone, appears in the christological hymn of 1 Timothy 3.16: 'He was . . . vindicated in spirit': God has rendered him justice. Once he had died on the cross without his God having lifted a finger, all his claims to be the evangelist, in words and deeds, of the divine kingship breaking through in the God-story, the final emissary of God into the world, had been wiped out not only in the eyes of his followers and his adversaries, but by God himself. The fact of his dying crucified meant that God had rejected him, the cross being also a theological symbol in the Jewish religious culture of the time: God could not be on the side of a crucified person, who was regarded as an evil-doer. Jesus in his horrendous death had been de-confessed by God, at least as everyone thought, including his disciples who fled into Galilee. Now the Easter event, expressed in juridical terms, demonstrated that God has rendered him justice, legitimizing him, proving him right. Trust can be placed in him; his earthly existence is revelatory of the divine.

All this makes clear that the resurrection of Jesus is not equivalent to bringing his corpse back to life. In the Gospels the raising of Lazarus and of Jairus' daughter were told as such. Real or invented, they were giving of life to corpses: those concerned resumed a life that had previously been ended in death. Jesus, though, did not *come back* to life but was raised by God as 'the living one' (Rev. 1.18), he who 'will never die again' (Rom. 6.9). He has received a new life overflowing with newness of life for us. His resurrection does not seem to be about what to do with his corpse, as moreover applies to the future resurrection of those who are in Christ. Not for nothing does Paul, a canny theologian, speak of corporeality, distinguishing between physical body, full of natural life, and 'spiritual' body – a contradiction in terms in Greek culture – completely filled with the Spirit (1 Cor. 15.42ff). The body is not part of the person, but the whole person understood as a being essentially in dialogue with God, with others, with the world. Because according to Paul, as Bultmann remarked, we do not have a body but are body. As risen, Christ is 'spiritual' body to the greatest power, concentrated with the vital energies of the Spirit of God.

IV. The gospel accounts of the empty tomb

In the confessions of faith dating from the first thirty years there is no mention of the empty tomb. An account of finding the tomb empty appears for the first time in Mark 16.1–8: the women who had witnessed Jesus' death on the cross and his burial, which set the seal on his death, went to the sepulchre on the morning after the Sabbath and found that the big stone that had closed off the entrance had been rolled away: what was hermetically closed had been opened. In Ezekiel 37.12 the people shut away in the land of their exile hear the word that communicates God's decision to 'raise up' the exiled people: 'I am going to open your graves, and bring you up from your graves, O my people; and I will bring you back to the land of Israel'. This is a powerful expression of the symbol: from the closure of the world of death to the opening to new life. The women then discover that Jesus' tomb is empty. This means that the realm of death now no longer contains the crucified Jesus, is empty of him who has been made to come out of it. Finally the women – and this is the true focus of the story – hear the divine announcement made by a heavenly messenger: 'You are looking for Jesus of Nazareth, who was crucified. He has been raised; he is not here' (v. 6). This metaphorical significance of the empty tomb is even clearer in the parallel account in Luke 24.5, in which the heavenly messengers – no longer one, but two – ask the perplexed women, 'Why do you look for the living among the dead?' Jesus is no longer one of the dead; he has escaped from them through the power of God. The empty tomb signifies precisely this going out from the realm of the dead, in its turn symbolized by the full tomb.

V. It was not a miracle of apologetic stamp

The resurrection of Jesus has too often been regarded as a miracle that justifies faith; but it is not like that: it rather forms the central nucleus of Christian faith: 'If Christ has not been raised' – and he is not the one who raises, we should add, in line with Paul's thinking – 'then our proclamation has been in vain and your faith has been in vain' (1 Cor. 15.14). This is to say that the experience of believing in him would have no value for salvation; and 'you are still in your sins', as the apostle goes on to say (v. 17). The same would be true of the gospel proclamation: it would not be the bearer of a truthful announcement of happiness on the part of God.

Those who rely on the late gospel narratives, Luke and John, fall into the same trap. At first sight, these appear to lean toward a material verification of the risen Jesus: he is touched (by Thomas, in John 20.24ff); he eats with his disciples (Luke 24.43). In reality these are apologetic accounts. At a certain point the Christians of the first century were impelled by denials on the part of the Jews to rise to the level of dialectical argument to promote their own faith in the face of opposition. And they did not split hairs: such accounts, not lacking in naivety, made use of diatribe to defend *the reality* of the resurrection of Jesus, *not his materiality*. It is not for nothing that John himself tells of Mary Magdalene that, having gone to the sepulchre, she meets someone in the garden whom she takes for the gardener – her eyes were conditioned to see not the reality but only appearances – and recognizes the Lord only when he calls her by her name (John 20.11ff). In the same way the disciples from Emmaus did not recognize the one who walked with them; he was not visibly recognizable; only with the eyes of faith did they recognize the Lord in the Eucharistic sign of the breaking of bread (Luke 24.13ff).

VI. The risen Christ inhabits the present of the human race

The experience undergone by Peter and companions is very similar to that of all believers, with this distinction, which does not thereby change the substance of the picture: they had lived with Jesus and had been able to see, in the spirit that encouraged them after the catastrophe of Good Friday, the Spirit *of Jesus*. They were able to express this by uniting their memories of the earthly Jesus with their new paschal experience, an experience of grace. This experience remains open as a real and non-illusory possibility to all human beings, and it is in fact undergone by all who truly anticipate, in their own lives, through grace, the final resurrection. Resurrection not only of individual persons, but also of groups and of peoples capable, through the grace of the Risen One, of un-nailing themselves from the wood of the cross and bringing life even to the realms of the dead. Because Jesus remains through time the raised one who raises.

The same horizon of 'actuality' opens out through the lordship of the risen Christ, lordship over the world (cf. the hymn in Phil.) and more directly over human lives – an exclusive, liberating, and gathering lordship. 'There are many gods and many lords' on earth, Paul says, referring to their presence in the lives of idolaters bending their knee before the world and the powers on this earth. From a world full, in this sense, of gods and lords, the believers' 'we' take a decisive distance: 'Yet *for us* there is one God, the Father . . . and one Lord, Jesus Christ' (1 Cor. 8.4–8). With the monotheism of the Hebrew tradition Paul combines the mono-lordship of Jesus, capable of banishing any other lordship from human lives. Still addressing the Corinthians, the apostle recommends: 'You were bought with a price; do not become slaves of human masters' (1 Cor. 7.23). Also, affirming Christ as 'the Lord' has meaning not in abstract affirmations about the life of the champion but in the life-experience of those who, to use a strong Pauline expression, become slaves of Christ (1 Cor. 7.22), as Paul repeatedly asserts of himself.

Translated by Paul Burns

Metaphysical Aspects of the Concept of Resurrection

THOMAS SCHÄRTL

Perhaps it will seem naïve or retrograde to confront the theological questions that cluster round the problem of Jesus' resurrection and topics associated with individual eschatology, with *metaphysical* questions. But a very basic hermeneutical perspective gives rises to these particular questions. Sooner or later, anyone who asks, 'What does resurrection mean?', expecting something more than a mere recital of biblical narratives, and anyone who takes a systematic-theological interest in the possibility of resurrection and inquires into what 'really happened' at Easter, will have to engage with metaphysical formulations of these questions. It is the qualification 'really' that does this by inviting us to reconcile the concept of resurrection with the way in which we understand reality.

I. The conceivability problem

But 'understanding reality' in itself makes the process of deciding what is meant by 'resurrection' extremely uncertain. If we had to find an appropriate term to describe the foremost contemporary metaphysical interpretation of the meaning of things, it would have to be 'naturalistic'. But what does 'naturalistic' mean? A set of axioms provided by Kai Nielsen, the Canadian critic of religion, may help us to arrive at some idea of what a naturalistic interpretation of the world might amount to.[1] The most important guiding principles are:

1. There is nothing apart from physical nature.
2. Everything there is, is of a physical nature or at least so constituted that it is associated with physical nature.
3. There is no supernatural reality, no spiritual-ethereal being, or any kind of independent, purely mental reality.

4. All objects are physical objects.
5. Human actions are individual events. The reason why these actions are carried out is, however, from another viewpoint, the cause of their occurrence.

At first sight, it would seem possible even for a theist to accept some of these principles, whereas others need more precise definition. Yet others will encounter open criticism – as is immediately evident, for instance, in the case of the first proposition. But the problem raised by naturalism is precisely one of varying interpretations of its basic principles. After all, a naturalist view of the world is compatible with theism up to a certain point. Essentially, the first and fifth propositions in the above list are the really problematical *cruces*. For a theist, God is a non-physical reality; therefore the first proposition is unacceptable to theists. On the other hand, it is another, specific question whether the consequences of the distinction between cause and reason adumbrated in the fifth proposition (which in certain respects requires a human being to be described in the same way as a spiritual-personal and as a corporeal being, as subject and object) are not also extremely problematical.

The complex of problems specific to naturalism emerges primarily when it tries to encompass more than is appropriate to its function as a practical scientific paradigm to be used for purposes of orientation. This is more or less the case when Kai Nielsen proffers the following judgment of theistic 'concepts of the afterlife' – especially with regard to hope of resurrection:

> Such stories depend for their intelligibility on being underdescribed. The more we, remaining stubbornly literal, try to fill them in, the more problematical they become, less coherent they seem. (Philosophers talk of the 'limits of intelligibility' but we have no clear idea of what we are talking about here.) Still, perhaps no contradictions are involved in their characterizations: problematicity and doubtful coherence yes, inconsistency no, or at least perhaps no. (Still, what is or isn't consistent is not easy to ascertain.) Where no disembodiment assumptions sneak in by the back door to carry the self from one body to the next, bodily resurrection seems at least to [be] some kind of obscure logical possibility. Still, that is not saying very much at all.[2]

But why should the idea of resurrection be no more than an obscure logical possibility? Surely we have already come a long way once we can confirm that resurrection is somehow 'conceivable'? Nielsen's verdict is based on a particular interpretation that imputes a kind of dualism to any notion of resurrection. In order to fill the gap in identity and continuity between death and a life after this one, we would have to posit a *non-corporeal soul* or a *disembodied person* that would guarantee this particular context. Nielsen has strong reservations about the acceptability of this idea, as adumbrated.[3]

Nielsen does talk of the logical possibility though metaphysical impossibility of the concept of a 'disembodied person'. Accordingly, he touches on a decisive, though also strongly contested, point in the contemporary confrontation with naturalism: the concept of that which is 'metaphysically possible'. In naturalism the notion of the 'metaphysically possible' is developed on the basis of the fundamental laws of our world – which means primarily those structural laws that can be extrapolated against the background of a scientific world-view. But recourse to the limited frame of reference afforded by a natural-scientific interpretation of the world would intolerably restrict any attempt to elicit what is possible. Essentially, what Nielsen understands as 'metaphysical possibility' is simply no more than 'what is possible in accordance with laws determined by the natural sciences'. A much older continental-European tradition (to some extent following Leibniz, and sometimes accused of a rationalist bent) would equate what is metaphysically possible with what is conceptually possible, and immediately proclaim a philosophical ukase against any concept that runs up against conceptual difficulties that declare it to be unintelligible. Yet this view relies on the conviction that a natural-scientific description of the world does not tell us everything about our world and reality, and that it possibly depends on a voluntarily restricted methodology that retains its justification and advantages only while it assists our reason in connection with a specific mode of orientation in the world.

In contradistinction to all forms of naturalist objection, the following remarks rely on the assurance that (a) resurrection is metaphysically possible; and (b) the concept of resurrection does not have to be associated with the concept of a disembodied person, as long as we do not understand the terms 'person' and 'bodily existence' in a restricted sense from the start.

2. The evidence problem

But perhaps the very question of the conceivability of resurrection is too dull, and possibly too uninteresting theologically speaking. Surely – precisely if we are concerned fundamental theologians – we have to ask why it is so important to retain the idea of resurrection. But what kind of evidence are we looking for? For instance, would the *probabilist* approach in any such argument, as suggested by Richard Swinburne,[4] be appropriate both to the inquiry formulated in the foregoing and to the substance of belief in resurrection? Is it enough to say that the resurrection of Jesus is very probable if the existence of a loving God who reveals himself to humans in human form is probable? Does a primary philosophical justification of belief in resurrection, as presented by Hansjürgen Verweyen, offer a better strategy – a demonstration that we shall be brought under the sway of belief in resurrection if we re-examine the concept of resurrection itself and learn from Jesus' destiny and cross to *see* the message for us of belief in the resurrection:[6] that is, that a true image of the absolute has been established in the midst of a multitude of false images, and that this, to the exclusion of all mere images, represents the sole true and authentic Image of the Absolute. But Verweyen's approach, too, is capricious, at least in the sense that he (a) not only replaces the concept of resurrection hermeneutically by an entirely different notion (that of 'being an image of the absolute'), but (b) ascribes to the cross the status of unambiguous, objective evidence that will also be able to offer certainty to later generations of believers. There is no consideration here of the fact that there is a hermeneutical, and also so to speak evidentially aesthetic, gulf between cross and resurrection; and that the cross, in itself, is far too ambivalent to provide the objective evidence in question.

What direction are we to take if we can rely *neither* on a probabilist line of argument, which seemingly treats belief in resurrection as if it were a scientific hypothesis, *nor* on uncovering some form of objective evidence? Perhaps the following remark of Wittgenstein's will prove helpful when considering this problem:

What inclines even me to believe in Christ's resurrection? It is as though I play with the thought: – If he did not rise from the dead, then he is decomposed in the grave like any other man. *He is dead and decomposed.* In that case he is a teacher like any other and can no longer *help*; and once more we are orphaned and alone. So we have to content ourselves with wisdom and speculation. We are in a sort of hell where we can do nothing but dream, roofed in, as it were, and cut off from heaven. But if I am to be *really* saved, what I need is *certainty* – not wisdom, dreams or speculations – and this certainty is faith. And faith is what is needed by my *heart*, my *soul*, not my speculative intelligence. For it is my soul with its passions, as it were with its flesh and blood, that has to be saved, not my abstract mind.

Perhaps we can say: Only *love* can believe the Resurrection. Or: It is *love* that believes the Resurrection. We might say: Redemptive love also believes in the Resurrection, also holds fast to the Resurrection. What combats doubt is, as it were, *redemption*. Holding fast to *it* has to be holding fast to this belief. And so that means: you need only be redeemed and hold fast to your redemption (abide by your redemption) – then you will see that you hold fast to this belief.[7]

This highly compressed train of thought takes us into existential territory from the start. If I know what redemption means, I shall be able to understand what resurrection means. The dimension of certainty is disclosed only by love. Ultimately it is the love that grants peace to the restless heart (here Wittgenstein refers to Augustine) that can conceive of belief in resurrection as credible and certain. Perhaps it is even possible to garner a hermeneutical advantage from this somewhat lyrical-sounding formulation. Belief in resurrection is a matter of perspective. There is probably no straightforwardly realistic understanding, no satisfactory translation, for the concept in question. What is intended here is perceptible to an anticipatory form of understanding from the perspective of hope of redemption. And it is this 'pre-understanding' that enables one to view the evidence required by belief in resurrection, for love knows how to perceive the difference between life and death as the basis of its certainty. Because love wants and affirms life, it finds its evidence in the statement 'Jesus is alive' precisely because, as love, it has unconditionally to want, and does unconditionally want, Jesus to be alive. This logic of love is a logic of absolute affirmation, which discovers the decisive criterion that verifies its unconditionality in the basic 'existential' encoding of the paired contraries 'death' and 'life'. The love that allows itself to envision redemption through the eyes of imagination 'knows' about the unconditionality of the life and the evidence of a message that has to do with life. What the New Testament so often represents as 'Easter' is the narrational and declarative form of expression of the statement: 'Jesus is alive'. It may be difficult to elucidate the difference between death and life on a even conceptual level, as it were; but it is perfectly comprehensible in a perspective of love that reaches out for redemption: life means being an addressee of a person's love, and at the same time being capable of loving, or of lovingly acknowledging, the other person in his or her own right. The whole meaning of the message of the resurrection depends on Jesus' life. If Jesus is to be proclaimed as the Christ, he cannot remain in the state of death.

The concept of 'life' is certainly difficult to grasp. Ultimately, perhaps, it cannot be defined exhaustively. In a perspective of hope of redemption, this term stands for a basic concept that is entirely reasonable in its own right, and unambiguously clear in its opposition to death. A dead person can no longer be a genuine recipient of my love, and cannot in any way decide, or have decided, to love me. If, accordingly, love loves beyond death, it 'knows' more, for it testifies to life.

Nevertheless – on a fundamental-theological basis – to remain satisfied with this perspective alone (from which, however, it is possible to develop a transcendental resurrection concept) is not a convincing resolution of our quest. After all, we are still left with the question (one that proceeds from a conceptual viewpoint, and from a conceptual logic, as it were) whether that which the perspective of redemption hopes for and the logic of love perceives as unconditionally certain, is also intelligible. Only if what is hoped for is not merely not incomprehensible, but also conceivable, and if what is perceived to be certain is also genuinely possible, is it justifiable to proclaim the news of resurrection as wholly credible. Conceivability does not supply any evidence; all that conceivability does is to show that what is hoped for is also truly possible.

All the same, *conceivability* is an important criterion. To surrender conceivability as a criterion of credibility is tantamount to adopting the reserve characteristic of the kind of criticism of religion met with in naturalist interpretations of the world. The meaning of 'resurrection' may defy definition, up to a point, yet the work of fundamental theology would be over before it had begun, if resurrection were to prove 'unintelligible'.

But what does 'resurrection' mean? What can a logic of love know? What can be known by virtue of this mode of 'knowing' that also asks to be recognized as intelligible? A formal suggestion for an explanation of the concept of life might take the following form: Resurrection means the actual existence of a person in spite of the break represented by death; talk of 'existence' reaches beyond a basic ontological significance to include the fact that the person in question can also exist in relation to other persons, and possesses all those characteristics that comprise what being a person is for a person. The exact definition of what those characteristics might be could be a topic of debate in more extensive discussions that can only be hinted at here. But – and this intimation *e contrario* will possibly suffice – can anything be said to be living if it does not possess cognitive, active, and interactive capacities?

3. The metaphysical problem: restitution – transformation – material realization

Accordingly, traditional theology was justifiably aware of 'resurrection' in metaphysical concepts and sought to read it in their lines. We can find a major echo of these considerations in the academic theological manuals of systematic theologians. Although to us nowadays the clarity of the way in which the concept is presented might seem *too clear* (and also too arid), and although close contemporary scrutiny might show that what was once so precisely defined is no longer so unambiguous, the traditional 'metaphysical translation' enjoying the status of a classic formula is certainly a starting-point for the appropriate train of thought in this case. Christ's resurrection indivisibly encompasses a dual aspect: '. . . the restoration of his bodily life by the reunion of body and soul, and the transfiguration of his body and of his life, so that the first is transfigured through the latter as Christ's second, higher birth: as the beginning, that is, of a new, higher life.'[8]

The scope of this definition, which originates with Matthias J. Scheeben, reaches a long way back, before medieval speculations, to resurrection concepts whose outlines we can already find in the Latin Fathers of the Church. Moreover this definition is an attempt to concentrate the 'polyphony'[8] of tradition in a single concept – which makes it highly inconsistent. In fact (like many exponents of tradition before him) Scheeben tries to yoke together the concepts of *restitution* and *transformation*. There is an echo of the *restitution concept* of resurrection in the model of the reunited body and soul. The *transformation concept* of resurrection is discernible in the notion of *metamorphosis*. The former plays on the idea of retrieved *integrity*; the latter on that of transition to a higher plane. The emphasis on a concept of integrity is understandable as soon as we realize that it conceals an attachment to the bodily nature of resurrection (and therefore an anti-Gnostic and anti-spiritualist tendency). The concept itself, however, is hopelessly indeterminate, and possibly definable only with great difficulty.[9]

In the event, the sought-after union of body-soul model affords even greater difficulties. At some point, any proponent of an *anima separata* conception has to argue on a dualist basis (essentially a dualism of substantiality),[10] and therefore has to handle problems culminating in one simple question that takes precedence of all conventional questions about body-soul dualism (such as interaction and upward or downward causation): Why does a *soul substance* not simply remain in a disembodied state after death? Is there any reason whatsoever why this entity should exist in or with a body? Or (more precisely): Is there any reason whatsoever why this entity should have existed in an embodied state? Traditional answers to this question sought to categorize the disembodied state of a soul as *defective*.[11] But what does an 'embodied' soul gain in terms of substantial characteristics if it is said already, as an *anima separata*, to possess cognitive capacities and the capacity of action?

But the decisively weak point of the dualist approach is probably the simple fact that it merely displaces the complex of problems associated with integrity. Admittedly, it is proposed that the soul might, as it were, vouch for the integrity or the restoration of integrity; but as soon as the soul is considered as an (even if only an intermittent) entity in its own right, the problems associated with integrity are also posed in respect of the soul. Platonizing talk of the soul's *simplicity* and *immutability* does not resolve this difficulty but merely circumvents it by adopting a strategy of immunization against precise definition, resulting ultimately in the stylization of the substance of the soul as a somewhat mysterious (and accordingly inaccessible) entity. To begin with, these theoretical difficulties force us to return to the notion of integrity and to seek a new way of determining integrity.

An alternative to the above-mentioned model construction would be the mereological approach by which a finite person is viewed as as a whole consisting of so many parts. This approach requires people to be seen as complex constructions, as living organisms, and tries to determine the criteria of *integrity* on that basis. But impossible conceptual difficulties arise as soon as we take the first steps into this territory. It is difficult enough trying to answer questions about integrity in respect of lifeless or artificial objects,[12] but it is just as hopeless to try to pin down integrity in living organisms that continually shed parts, and accumulate and assimilate others, without recourse to a quest for a concept of *structure* or *form* more or less in the Aristotelian tradition.

Since it is scarcely possible to determine the integrity of a living organism 'from below', that is, by calculating the sum of its parts, we can solve the problem of integrity (if at all) only if we admit that the sole reason why an organism possesses integrity is that a *structure* holds the parts together 'from above'. But then the point maintained by restitution theory – the *re-assembly* of the *parts* that with death are lost or scattered, or decay – becomes a futile or meaningless requirement. For the result of any such restitution would be no more than a *copy* of a specific state of a former living entity.

The difficulties met with when we try to determine the concept of integrity without logical disjunctions make a restitution concept of resurrection seem a very dubious proposition. Sooner or later, if we persist in seeking to establish the intelligibility of resurrection without any concomitant absurdities,[13] we have to propound a *transformation theory* of resurrection. The decisive aspect of this notion of resurrection is not the idea of integrity but the concept of identity, which – so long as it is not propounded rigidly[14] – is a much more flexible criterion than the concept of integrity. In this respect, care must be taken to ensure that the identity concept is backed up, as it were, by two mutually supportive criteria: by *continuity* and by *likeness*.[15] Whether we use them as mutually supportive facilities, or permit one to stand for the other on occasion, the application of both criteria will allow us to determine a person's identity throughout the changes wrought by time.

But to which 'areas' must we apply the criteria in question? Discussions about the problematical notion of personal identity have shown that neither concentration on purely physical and bodily characteristics nor focussing on entirely mental features or states is sufficient. They have also shown that a mixture of both criteria is not enough of itself, for it is possible to imagine cases in which the *testimony* of others must also be taken into account, in order to make up for presumed gaps in continuity at some other point. The inner dynamics of the identity concept also makes it conceivable that criteria should not only bear one another out reciprocally but be capable of replacing each other in extreme cases. Even if someone has entirely lost his or her memory and cognitive capacities, we can identify that individual (by, say, physical features); on the other hand, we ascribe an identity to someone even when he or she has undergone considerable physical change.

A dynamic approach to the concept of identity – dynamic because we do not have to look for support to one criterion and to one area exclusively – enables us to conceive of the notion of resurrection as transformation free from all contradiction. In this case, of course, the criterion of continuity is a very equivocal problem: *If we concede the intervention of a complete break in continuity in a person's existence between death and new life, the concept of identity collapses and we are thrown back on the ultimately ludicrous idea of restitution.* Therefore the only consistent solution must be to conceive of resurrection as '*transformation in death*'.[16] Or, in accordance with modern ontological usage: At the moment of death of a person P_1 in a world w_1, in a world w_2 a person P_2 emerges who, by the criteria of likeness and continuity, appears to be *identical* with P_1. Although in w_1 the corpse of person P_1 rots in the grave, it is possible for P_2 to be identical with P_1 if we accept criteria of identity which – *from the viewpoint of time* – allow of an '*identity leap*': Because P_2, unlike the corpse lying in the grave, is more like person P_1, and because there is a (for example, mental) relation of continuity between P_1 and P_2, the corpse in death can no longer be identical with the person P_1.[17]

Admittedly, to some extent the solution is dualist if we accept a difference in ontological status between a structure or a form and that which is structured or formed, since – and this should be evident from the so-called *material constitution* debate[18] – a structure is *not identical* with its material manifestation. The relation of a structure to a material substrate is that of execution or of constitution (there is no other). Nevertheless, to say this does not mean that there is any such thing as an unachieved structure (in a *full* sense of 'there is'). That, indeed, would amount to an ontologically impoverished revival of the traditional *anima separata* theory. The decisive point lies elsewhere: If it is *conceivable* that a structure could be executed as different substrates, it is also *conceivable* that the material manifestation of a person P_2 in w_2 is a different manifestation to that of P_1 in w_1, and yet that P_2 is identical with P_1, because the *structure* so to speak remains 'the same' (that is, satisfies pertinent criteria with regard to likeness and continuity).[19]

But surely we are still faced with the problem of having to explain away the corpse as if it were some kind of leftover ontological refuse? On closer examination, it is clear that the question can be posed in that way only from the viewpoint of restitution theory. Nevertheless, present-day systematic theologians should stop getting into knots over an idea that, on closer scrutiny, is evidently totally absurd or irremediably complicated. Since (and if) the corpse is no longer identical with the person under discussion, why should we pay it any more attention – over and above, that is, the modicum of pious respect that we accord a dead body because traces of the departed are still evident in it? In the end, any such piety deserves the corrective judgment: 'You seek the living among the dead'. And we shall certainly not find the living there.

But that, surely, is no more than a subtle excuse for invoking a Christianized form of spiritualism? This question, too, can be posed only if we discern the human frame in the corpse, and the living body itself in the frame. But of course the sequence of supposedly equivalent substantives ('corpse', 'human frame', 'living body') is highly problematical. Then, as philosophies in the phenomenological tradition would suppose they have demonstrated conclusively, corporeality is a condition of the finite *mind* – it is the *external aspect*[20] of the finite mind, its passiveness, its susceptibility, its being called and its relatedness; accordingly it is to be located at the level of what I have already tentatively termed 'form' and 'structure'.

Then we still have to answer the question of what constitutes the support and basis of *continuity*. Taking an *attested* identity into account – that is, an identity associated with continuity and likeness – would allow us to move beyond the compass of an entirely mental continuity. But who would the 'eschatologically trustworthy' witness to this identity be? At this point, a necessarily theological aspect of the notion of resurrection comes into play: the conceivability of the resurrection concept is considerably increased if we agree to cite God as the privileged witness to our identity, and thus as the support and basis of continuity – though without resorting to a *deus ex machina* argument. If we are to avoid that particular solution, God must be the given ground of identity who was already and always present. But how exactly is that conceivable?

Our search for an answer leads back to the path of the traditional doctrine of immortality in its idealist manifestations.[21] Because finite subjects are always already 'immersed in God', and because we always already share in his absolute life, it is possible to conceive of a transformation in the moment of death that is empowered 'from above'.

We may summarize all the foregoing as follows: 1. It is possible to conceive of resurrection consistently if we consider it as *transformation in death*. 2. Resurrection becomes conceivable without having to represent it as a miracle pure and simple worked by God the almighty magician, if we finally discard the crude concept of restitution yet retain insights furnished by the material-constitution debate and subject them to critical scrutiny. 3. If we follow the lines of idealist and phenomenological philosophy and dare to conceive of our physicality as the *passibility* of finite subjectivity, which already, for its part, and in its own identity, has always been grounded in God in the sense of participation, then we must stop speculating about the full or empty state of the graves of resurrected people, because all we would find in them anyway would be corpses, and not persons who are spiritually endowed subjects open to others.

Translated by J. G. Cumming

Notes

1. Cf. on this point Kai Nielsen, 1996, *Naturalism without Foundations*, Amherst, New York, p. 35.
2. *Idem*, 1981, *Naturalism and Religion*, Amherst, New York, p. 81.
3. *Ibid.*, p. 93.
4. See Richard Swinburne, 2003, *The Resurrection of God Incarnate*, Oxford and New York, pp. 9–31, 201–3.

5. Cf. Hansjürgen Verweyen, ³2000, *Gottes letztes Wort. Grundriss der Fundamentaltheologie*, Regensburg, esp. the 'Easter theses', pp. 341–7.
6. Ludwig Wittgenstein, ⁴1990, 'Vermischte Bemerkungen', in Ludwig Wittgenstein, *Werkausgabe*, Vol. 8, Frankfurt, pp. 445–573, esp. 495f.
7. Matthias J. Scheeben, 1882, ²1925, *Handbuch der katholischen Dogmatik*, Vol. 3, Freiburg, p. 303.
8. On multiple opinions see the useful comments in Caroline W. Bynum, 1995, *The Resurrection of the Body in Western Christianity (200–1336)*, New York.
9. Peter Simons, 1987, *Parts. A Study in Ontology*, Oxford, pp. 326–35.
10. An explicit reworking of *dualist* models for eschatological questions is to be found in contemporary philosophy, especially in Richard Swinburne, and recently in Uwe Meixner, who offers an eschatological extension of the basic outlines he has already provided within the limits of purely metaphysical considerations: U. Meixner, 2004, *The Two Sides of Being. A Reassessment of Psycho-Physical Dualism*, Paderborn; see also R. Swinburne, 'Personal Identity: The Dualist Theory', in Sidney Shoemaker & Richard Swinburne, 1984, *Personal Identity*, Oxford, pp. 1-66. See further, esp. on other attempts at adaptation, John W. Cooper, 1989, ²2000, *Body, Soul and Life Everlasting. Biblical Anthropology and the Monism-Dualism Debate*, Grand Rapids and Cambridge.
11. On the revival of categories of this kind, see Stephen T. Davis, 1993, *Risen Indeed. Making Sense of the Resurrection*, Grand Rapids.
12. Cf. Trenton Merricks, 2001, *Objects and Persons*, Oxford, esp. pp. 2–29. See also Peter van Inwagen, 1990, *Material Beings*, Ithaca, New York, esp. pp. 81–97.
13. Cf. in this respect John Perry, 1978, *A Dialogue on Personal Identity and Immortality*, Indianapolis; also Ted Peters, 'Resurrection. The Conceptual Challenge', in Ted Peters, Robert John Russell & Michael Welker (eds.), 2002, *Resurrection. Theological and Scientific Assessments*, Grand Rapids and Cambridge, pp. 297–321.
14. I find too inflexible the notion of identity that leads Parfit to exclude the identity concept: Derek Parfit, 1984, ²1986, *Reasons and Persons*, Oxford, esp. pp. 281–306.
15. For a dynamic concept of identity see Robert Nozick's so-called closest-continuer theory, which has become something of a modern classic: R. Nozick, 1981, *Philosophical Explanations*, Oxford, pp. 43–70. Cf. Harold Noonan, 1989, *Personal Identity*, London & New York, pp. 154–62, 233–54.
16. Ulrich Lüke, 'Auferstehung am Jüngsten Tag als Auferstehung im Tod', in: *StZ* 216 (1998), 45–54.
17. Cf. in this regard Hud Hudson, 2001, *A Materialistic Metaphysics of the Human Person*, Ithaca & London, pp. 167–92.
18. For a more extensive treatment see Lynn Rudder Baker, 2000, *Persons and Bodies. A Constitution View*, Cambridge, and further Christopher M. Brown,

n.d., *Aquinas and the Ship of Theseus. Solving Puzzles about Material Objects*, London & New York, esp. pp. 16–47.

19. The relevant detailed questions were treated traditionally under the headword 'Auferstehungsleib' (lit. 'risen body' or 'resurrected body'). There is a noteworthy contribution in this respect by the young Joseph Ratzinger in *Lexikon für Theologie und Kirche*., He supports a very open version of the principle of material realization and thus counters not only a crude materialism but any too attenuated form of realization theory. See J. Ratzinger, 'Auferstehungsleib', in: LThK¹, Vol. 1, cols. 1052f.

20. See in this regard the comments on Levinas in Josef Wohlmuth, 2005, *Mysterium der Verwandlung. Eine Eschatologie aus katholischer Perspektive im Gespräch mit jüdischem Denken der Gegenwart*, Paderborn, pp. 183f.

21. See Georg W. F. Hegel, 1995, *Die vollendete Religion – nach der Vorlesung von 1824*, in idem: *Vorlesungen über die Philosophie der Religion*. Part 3: *Die vollendete Religion*. W. Jaeschke (ed.), Hamburg, pp. 99–176, esp. 140. Cf also Johann G. Fichte, 1971, *Die Bestimmung des Menschen*, in: *Fichtes Werke*, I. H. Fichte (ed.), Vol. II: *Zur theoretischen Philosophie* II, Berlin, pp. 165–319, esp. 317f.

III. Resurrection in Present Life

The Resurrection of Nature: an Aspect of Cosmic Christology

JÜRGEN MOLTMANN

I. Resurrection of the dead and abrogation of death

The historicity of Jesus' resurrection has been the central problem of theology since the beginning of the modern era because 'history' has become the major paradigm of the modern world.[1] 'History', however, has been applied to the human world as distinct from ahistorical nature. Then 'history' must be understood as the realm of freedom, and nature as that of statutory necessity. But this distinction implies a human mind (or spirit) deprived of any natural embodiment, and a nature without mind (or spirit). Medicine has been the only area in which reality is not divided along these lines.

Every woman and every man is a physical and mental whole, for mind and nature are inseparably united in human existence. 'History' in the sense of the modern paradigm is inappropriate to the physical and accordingly natural existence of human beings. We need a new paradigm to conceive the whole of reality and the unity of human existence proficiently. This new paradigm must unite psychosomatic and ecological aspects and thus comprehend the interaction and mutual interpenetration of human culture and the nature of the earth.[2]

If we examine the basis and strength of Christian belief in resurrection in this perspective, we have to transform historical Christology into a new, natural or ecological Christology and understand the personal experience of salvation psychosomatically. In so doing we resort to the traditional church doctrine of 'two natures' in Christology and see in Christ human nature accepted and permeated by divine nature. A basic tenet of that ancient doctrine is that 'what is not accepted cannot be saved'. Salvation is the salvation of creation as a whole and of all creatures and cannot be restricted to the salvation of the human soul or the salvation of human existence. Ultimately, human beings cannot be saved unless nature is saved, for humans are natural beings.

From the viewpoint of human history, the 'resurrection of Christ from the dead' means that the general resurrection of the dead has begun in him and with him. He is the first-fruits of those who have departed this life and the first-born among the dead. But that is only the personal aspect of resurrection. From the viewpoint of nature, the resurrection of Christ from the dead means that with him the universal 'deposition of death' (1 Cor. 15.26) has begun, and the future of the new creation of all things is visible in which 'there shall be an end to death' (Rev. 21.4). That is the cosmic aspect of hope of resurrection. The anti-God and destructive forces of sin and death will be expelled from God's good creation, which will become a creation with eternal life in the presence of the living God. In philosophical terms, we might say that the indestructible position of the positive proceeds only from the negation of the negative.

To understand this cosmic aspect of Christ's resurrection from death more proficiently, we must pause for a moment to consider the New Testament Easter narratives.[3] Jesus' disciples were frightened and fled when Jesus, in whom they had placed their entire messianic hope, died on the cross powerless and abandoned by God. 'But we had been hoping that he was to be the liberator of Israel', said the disciples in Emmaus (Luke 24.21). His death was the greatest disappointment of their lives. They betrayed, denied, and abandoned the one by whom they felt they had been betrayed and abandoned. But the other disciples, the women who had followed Jesus, remained loyal to the dying man and 'were also present, watching from a distance'. Some of them are also mentioned by name (Mark 15.40). For them, clearly, the observation of dying and death was not alien. They went to the grave of their friend and master when the Sabbath was over. They found the tomb empty and heard the angel say: 'He has been raised' (Mark 16.6). It was only at this point that they were afraid and ran away, trembling with amazement. Why? Birth and death are normal features of life on this earth, but Jesus' resurrection shattered the regular order of things.[4]

Moreover, death was no longer visible. The disappointment of the disciples' vital hope and the shock of the women who had seen where Jesus was laid were banished only by the appearances of the risen Jesus, who summons men and women to believe in the new reality that he embodies (Mark 16.14; John 20.27).

Therefore Jesus 'resurrection' is to be interpreted not only as God's eschatological and historical action, but as the first achievement of this transient world as recreated in its true and everlasting form. Resurrection is the meaning not merely of history but of nature. The consequence for the new human life lived in the presence of the risen Christ is expectation of the 'resurrection of the flesh'.[5] As is shown by references to the pouring out of the life-giving Spirit 'upon all flesh' (Joel 2.28; Acts 17), 'flesh' in Hebrew usage means everything that has life (*kol basar*). The action of the Spirit of resurrection that gives 'new life to your mortal bodies' (Rom 8.11) is not limited to human individuals but includes the whole living world in which humans exist physically. 'Up to the present, as we know, the whole created universe in all its parts groans as if in the pangs of childbirth. What is more, we also, to whom the Spirit is given as the first-fruits of the harvest to come, are groaning inwardly while we look forward eagerly to our adoption, our liberation from mortality' (Rom. 8.22, 23).

Expectation of the resurrection of the flesh takes us into the fullness of life in this world. As our love is directed to life, we can expend and sacrifice ourselves entirely, for nothing is in vain, nothing decays, and in the resurrection everything will be restored. Without belief in resurrection it is impossible to reconcile a life of love with death.[6] We can see what is meant by that reconciliation if we consider the image of the seed that is bare and solitary, that is, dead and unfruitful, until it is sown in the earth. Then 'it dies', that is, changes into the plant that yields a great amount of fruit (1 Cor. 15.36–44): 'What is sown as a perishable thing is raised imperishable'. Life that is truly alive is a seed of love in the power of hope of resurrection.

II. Resurrection – meaning of nature

By 'nature' we understand the present condition of the disordered creation, which is replete with beautiful things but also with disasters. Yet we interpret this nature as God's creation because we trust in the loyalty of its Creator and see how, in respect of his aims, it can be transformed. What has Christ to do with nature? Paul already talks of Christ's mediation of creation: 'Yet for us there is one God, the Father, from whom are all things, and we exist for him; there is one Lord, Jesus Christ, through whom are all things, and we exist through him' (1 Cor. 8.6). If all things exist 'through Christ', then not only the Messiah of history but the wisdom of the whole creation, as it was made originally, is revealed in him. But that means precisely that the first Christians saw Christ in all natural things and all natural things in Christ. The resulting cosmic spirituality is described in the well-known *logion* 77 of the apocryphal Gospel of Thomas. There Christ says:

> I am the light set over all things.
> I am the universe; the universe proceeded from me
> and the universe returns to me.
> Split a piece of wood, and I am there.
> Pick up a stone and you will find me.[7]

Consequently, the powers of nature were to be honoured as gods as little as the idols of the human world, as the emperor, or capital (1 Cor. 8,1–13). The sun, moon, and stars are good elements of creation, but they are not themselves gods. Under the rule of the risen Christ, people will be liberated from the divinization of natural forces and from fear of them. Christ reconciles humans to God's good creation. Orientation to the forces of nature, which are themselves in need of redemption, is pointless.

The basis for recognition of the cosmic Christ is to be found in the Easter appearances of the risen Jesus. What was perceived in his appearances extends beyond all historical experiences and seems to be the very existence of creation itself. The God who calls the dead into life is the same God who called into being all things that were not (Rom. 4.17); and the God who raised Jesus from the dead is the Creator of the new existence of all things. Resurrection and creation belong together, since the resurrection of the dead and the annihilation of death are the fulfilment of the original creation. Even at a very early stage, the light of the Easter appearances was seen as the dawn light of the first day of the new creation of all things. Later on Sunday was also known as the 'eighth day', because it was celebrated as the day of resurrection. In the light of this new day created by God Christ appears as the first-born of the whole creation (Col. 1.15), who 'reconciles' everything in heaven and on earth (Col. 1.20) and will redeem all things. The 'first to return from the dead' (Col. 1.18) is also the one who enjoys 'primacy over all creation' (Col. 1.15), through whom all things were made.

In practice this cosmic Christology means that the Christian communities in the multi-religious towns of the ancient world did not present themselves as comprising just one of the many religious communities of a hitherto unrecognized divinity, but as the community of the Creator and Redeemer of all things, and as one establishing peace and unity. What they wanted was not a new religion but a new world. They did not provide a new cult but new life. They did not offer competition between religions, for their missionary task was to achieve the peace of the cosmos and the reconciliation of humankind. The Christ whom they proclaimed was honoured not only as the Lord of the faithful but as the wisdom of the entire creation, and he was awaited as the redeemer of nature. The Church sees itself as the beginning of the reconciled cosmos and as anticipating the new universal creation. In this respect it is a microcosmic image of the macrocosm that is destined to be the temple of God. This does not imply that the world is to be made ecclesiastical through and through, but that the cosmic dimensions of Christ are to be anticipated. As the body of Christ, the Church already represents the entire creation. 'The Most High does not live in houses made by men; as the prophet says: "Heaven is my throne and earth my footstool. What kind of house will you build for me, says the Lord; where shall my resting-place be? Are not all these things of my own making?"' (Acts 7.48–50; cf. Is. 66.1-2). God is worshipped in the temple of his creation whole and entire. Every church, cathedral, and Christian edifice is built with that in mind. Only in its function as a home for all creation is a Christian parish or community anything more than just one religious group among so many others. If Christ is not acknowledged as the wisdom of creation in all natural things, he is not duly acknowledged in the Church either. Christianity is intended to be the restorative beginning of a healthy and wholesome creation in the midst of a sick and shattered world. That is the joyful experience of the faithful: 'For anyone united to Christ, there is a new creation: the old order has gone; a new order has already begun' (2 Cor. 5.17).

III. Matter with a future

The first Enlightenment of the eighteenth century recommended a simple, mechanically-conceived materialism, not only heeding Descartes in his representation of the objective world in a purely geometrical manner as *res extensa*, but following Lamettrie in his conception of the human being as a machine. The nineteenth century, however, produced a new dialectical materialism. This approach tried to reconcile the human subject and nature as the object, in order to conceive of humankind in an appropriately natural, and nature in an appropriately human, way. When the young Marx writes: 'Motion is the first and supreme of the innate characteristics of matter, not only as mechanical and mathematical movement, but much more so as impulse, vital spirit, energy, and anguish – to use Jakob Böhme's term – of matter', there are unmistakable echoes of the Pauline image (Rom. 8) of creation groaning and longing.[8] Twentieth-century Marxist philosophers such as Ernst Bloch and Robert Havemann developed this Romantic idea of matter in terms of open-systems theory and process philosophy.[9] As Goethe put it, matter is form, moulded yet vitally evolving. Matter is not merely immediately available reality, for it is also, and always, its own potentiality. The forms it takes are not fixed in such a way that their content can be apprehended statically, but are apparent in the movements of communicative and anticipatory processes engaged in together with other material forms. Every determination of a state of matter is a human entry into an open process. Matter is subject to the processes of its ongoing transformation with a determinate past and an as yet indeterminate future. Accordingly Bloch's notion of a 'processual matter' fits the case. All shaped matter – and we know no other form of matter – is matter with a future. But what is its future?

The modern sciences interpret nature on the basis of anthropocentric interests. The nature of the earth should become a home for humankind and human beings should be seen as inhabitants of the earth. Nature should discover its future in the culture of the humanity that governs, uses, and preserves it. Nowadays the authentic symbols of nature, known traditionally as *signatura rerum*, are considered and processed as information and interpreted anthropocentrically. But is it possible to overcome the alienation between humankind and nature if present-day humans are alienated from themselves and they are unable to discern and acknowledge their own essential nature? People who are alienated from their very own selves will be unable to live in unison with nature.

Natural theology has always read the 'book of nature' theocentrically and eschatologically. All created things point to their Creator: 'The heavens sing the praises of the Eternal'. They also point beyond themselves into the future of their redemption in their true and permanent form in the kingdom of God. Human beings, too, are God's creations, and are oriented to the future of his kingdom as their everlasting home: 'What we shall be has not been disclosed, but we know that when Christ appears we shall be like him, because we shall see him as he is' (1 John 3.2). This does not result in any kind of historically attainable and ultimate community of humankind and nature, but in a historically anticipatory community on its way to and in consideration of a common future in the new universal creation in which all things will assume their authentic form in the kingdom of God. People who long for the 'redemption of the flesh' will join in community with all those creatures that groan under the burden of transience and long for God's glory. Cosmologists and anthropologists decipher the *signatura rerum* by recourse to an eschatological hermeneutics. This allows us to elicit the significance of nature in the light of its transcendent resurrection.

IV. The 'resurrection of nature'

The young Karl Marx had this vision of the meaning and goal of the history of the world: 'Therefore *society* is the complete existential unity of humankind and nature, the authentic resurrection of nature, the achieved naturalism of humankind and the achieved humanism of nature'.[10] He was able to conceive of nature as redeemed from its state of alienation only in terms of its resurrection in the world of humankind. But he did not see that as the extended human domination of nature and its subjection to human will, but as a mutual interpenetration of humankind and nature. Without the naturalism of humanity there was no humanism of nature, and without the humanism of nature there was no naturalization of humanity. But this essential unity of humankind and nature was to appear in the perfect, classless society free from domination. Authentic communism was to overcome not only the contradictions in human society but the contradictions between humans and nature, and even the contradictions in nature itself. Otherwise the term 'resurrection of nature' would be meaningless. Nevertheless, the young Marx underestimated the strength of evil and the power of death. Like Ludwig Feuerbach, he was an idealist who denied evil and ignored death. He must have known, however, when he wrote of resurrection, that resurrection presumes the existence of death, or else it could not defeat it. A 'humanism of nature' is not the 'resurrection of nature', but only the appropriation of nature by human beings. This, as is shown by the failed Soviet experiment and the now failing global experiment of capitalism, does not lead to the resurrection of nature but to its death. The Chernobyl disaster and the advancing catastrophe of climate change are the signs of our times.

But if a resurrection of nature in a society of mortal human beings is inconceivable, where can such a resurrection take the natural world? Traditionally, we think of a realm beyond this world in a heaven populated by the blessed, or an Elysium of pure spirits. But that is closer to Plato than to Jesus and the New Testament. The resurrection of the dead takes place on this earth and leads those who are given life, 'relying on his promise . . . to new heavens and a new earth, in which justice will be established' (2 Pet. 3.13). The kingdom of God is not a kingdom in heaven but comes about 'in heaven as on earth'. Resurrection and eternal life are God's promises for the people of this earth. Therefore a resurrection of nature will lead not into the next world but into this world renewed as the new creation of all things. God does not redeem his creation by establishing it in heaven, but renews the earth. 'God's kingdom is the realm of resurrection on earth.'[11] That means that all those who hope for resurrection are obliged to remain loyal to the earth, to care for it and to love it like themselves. The earth is the location of the coming kingdom of God, and therefore resurrection in the kingdom of God is the hope of this earth. The cross of Christ stood on this blood-soaked earth. Therefore God remains loyal to it and will banish pain, suffering, and death from it, in order to dwell there himself (Rev. 21.3, 4).

Does the created world offer any signs of this future of resurrection? I believe that all created things are created in anticipation of this future, for the fulfilment of creation 'in the beginning' is the celebration of creation in God's Sabbath of creation. God blesses all his creatures by his peace-giving presence. On the Sabbath he is present to all things. It is the Sabbath that distinguishes the idea of creation from the concept of nature. A Sabbatarian doctrine of creation is directed to the fulfilment of the created world in the eternal presence of God. The resurrection of the dead, the annihilation of death, and the resurrection of nature are the prerequisites for the everlasting creation that shares in the indwelling of the everlasting God. The creation 'in the beginning' is directed to this end. Accordingly, 'as we know, the whole created universe in all its parts groans [with us] as if in the pangs of childbirth' (Rom. 8.22). That is the true resurrection of nature.

Translated by J. G. Cumming

Notes

1. W. Pannenberg, 1964, *Grundzüge der Christologie*, Gütersloh.
2. J. Moltmann, 1989, *Der Weg Jesu Christi. Christologie in messianischen Dimensionen*, Munich; idem, 'Resurrection: The Ground, Power and Goal of our Hope', *Concilium* 1995/1, pp. 81–9.
3. T. Peters, R. Russell and M. Welcker (eds), 2002, *Resurrection. Theological and scientific assessments*, Grand Rapids. H.-J. Eckstein and M. Welcker, 2004, *Die Wirklichkeit der Auferstehung*, Neukirchen; T. Lorenzen, 2003, *Resurrection – Discipleship – Justice*, Macon, Georgia.
4. D. Juel indicated this emphatically in: J. Polkinghorne and M. Welcker (eds), 2000, *The End of the World and the Ends of God*, Harrisburg, p. 181.
5. E. Moltmann-Wendel and J. Moltmann, 2006, 'Mit allen Sinnen glauben: Auferstehung des Fleisches', in: *Leidenschaft für Gott. Worauf es uns ankommt*, Freiburg, pp. 22–43.
6. N. O. Brown, 1959, 'The Resurrection of the Body' in: *Life against Death. The Psychoanalytical Meaning of History*, New York, pp. 307ff.
7. E. Hennecke and W. Schneemelcher, 1968, *Neutestamentliche Apokryphen*, I. *Evangelien*, Tübingen, p. 213.

8. K. Marx, *Die Frühschriften*, S. Landshut (ed.), 1953, Stuttgart, p. 330.
9. E. Bloch, 1959, *Das Prinzip Hoffnung*, Frankfurt, ch. 17: 'Die Welt, worin utopische Phantasie ihr Korrelat hat', pp. 224–58.
10. Marx, *op. cit. supra*, p. 237. See also p. 235: 'This communism is . . .the authentic termination of the conflict between humanity and nature. . . . It is the puzzle of history solved, and acknowledges the resolution it provides'.
11. D. Bonhoeffer, 1958, *Dein Reich komme. Das Gebet der Gemeinde um Gottes Reich auf Erden*, Hamburg, p. 12. Christoph Blumhardt's influence on Bonhoeffer is easily recognizable here. Cf. L. Ragaz, 'Der Kampf um das Reich Gottes', in Blumhardt, 1922, *Vater und Sohn*, Zürich and Munich, esp. IV, 1: *Das Reich Gottes für die Erde*, pp. 44–62.

Resurrection as Process of a New Life

MÁRCIO FABRI DOS ANJOS

There are many aspects to consider in the theme of resurrection. Furthermore, there is a broader context of presuppositions in which reflection on the subject is situated. In this essay I am taking up a particular aspect, which consists in exploring the moral dimension of resurrection. This is not just a matter of expounding moral development coherent with faith in the resurrection, but rather an attempt to reflect on resurrection itself as a great process of moral transformation. Morality is therefore understood here as beyond its meaning of customs and modes of behaviour. It rather expresses the true ethical personality that forms persons through their free choices and responsibilities. My precise wish would be to insert it in this way in the process of becoming fully human, so as to reach a state of 'grace according to the measure of Christ's gift' (Eph. 4.7).

I am conscious of the fact that choosing this focus on the theme means that not all aspects of resurrection can be considered here, so this article needs to be read in conjunction with others in this issue. Given the limitations, I have chosen to indicate the broad lines of discussion on the subject and not quote chapter and verse on every point. I have thought it appropriate to stick basically to insights in biblical theology. My starting point, however, is anthropological, situating resurrection within the horizon of the human quest for survival.[1]

I. The worrying question of survival

From the anthropological point of view, resurrection is seen against the backdrop of the great challenge of human survival in the face of threats in life and the undeniable fact of death – how, then, to survive in life and how to survive, if possible, after death. In broad terms, the ancient Israelites placed the solution to these questions in their descendants. On the one hand, children meant a productive force (basically agricultural) and a force of political support to defend the lives of the group and its members, providing a means to feed them during struggles among clans and social disputes within the nation. Psalm 126 expresses this succinctly: 'Sons indeed are a heritage from the Lord, the fruit of the womb a reward. Like arrows in the hand of a warrior [the defensive force in war] are the sons of one's youth. Happy is the man who has his quiver full of them [production]. He shall not be put to shame when he speaks with his enemies in the gate [force to defend his political rights]' (vv. 3–5).

On the other hand, even if life in the midst of conflicts can be assured, what can be said of inevitable death, even at the end of a long life? Early Israel did not see the answer to this in terms of resurrection. Generally speaking, it saw survival after death in terms of the *memory* kept by descendants of their deceased ancestors. In other words, life goes on through being 'remembered from generation to generation'. It is interesting to note the concern to establish a framework for this remembrance in the pre-exilic period. In Genesis 23, for example, Abraham buys a field with a cave in which to bury Sarah, trying to guarantee the place for remembrance of ancestors and the sacred, and where he himself will be buried by Isaac and Ishmael (Gen. 25.9). This text is important for building a frame of reference for death and remembrance for those groups that in the period of Assyrian and Babylonian conquest were losing their identity and their cultural roots. This leads to the further note that the survival of ancestors in memory was also a question of the life of the people, since memory of their ancestors formed part of a great project of rebuilding their tradition.

The real and overwhelming experience of death that surrounds the life of the people and of individuals leads at the same time to seeking refuge in the faithfulness of God, to whom they are faithful: God will not 'let [his] faithful one see the Pit'.[2] This aspect of God's fidelity in guaranteeing the survival of the people underwent a particular time of crisis in Israel's confrontation with the great empires, with invasions, exile, and post-exile. On the one hand, the people were clearly not capable of guaranteeing their memory in the midst of the deportation and extermination of their own descendants; on the other, there was the enormous cultural impact of other concepts deriving from contact with the Persian, Greek, and Roman empires. Such experiences interfered with the people's culture and their efforts to understand life, history, and the world. The division between body and soul and the whole discourse of life after death, which emerged from contact with these cultures, receive strongly critical consideration in the wisdom of the Preacher (see esp. Eccl. 3).

The appeal to God's faithfulness to those who are faithful to him is re-affirmed in these contexts. 'The righteous live by their faith', Habakkuk was to say on the eve of the invasions (Hab. 2.4; cf. Rom. 1.17; Gal. 3.11; Heb. 10.38). The powerful context in which this prophet draws this conclusion is far from affirming faith in God's faithfulness as passivity and accommodation. In the quest for their survival, the righteous see themselves as and claim to be 'the fundamental and indispensable mediation of that divine intervention they cry out for. They are the only ones who are the powerful, transforming hand of the God who becomes visible, touchable, and active in history'.[3] The theology of martyrdom elaborated by the Maccabees clearly brings out the way that confidence in God's faithfulness opens to hope in eternal life, notwithstanding the imminence of death. But this hope also becomes a source of endurance and strength for individuals and groups. The unjust suffer a different fate, as can be seen in the account of the death of the mother and her seven Maccabee sons, compared to the death of the tyrant (compare, e.g., 2 Macc. 8 and 2 Macc. 9).

Within our concerns here, and also within the limits of this article, it is worth introducing a short note on *immortality*. As is known, this Hellenic concept appears late in the Wisdom of Solomon; it is less important in Hebraic culture and in the New Testament, but it gains importance in Christian thought particularly through its use by the Fathers from the second century on. Briefly, the Book of Wisdom, 'making use of the Platonic teachings on the distinction between body and soul (cf. 9.15) and on the immortality of the soul, states that God made us for incorruption (2.23), that the reward for wisdom is that incorruption which assures us a place near to God (6.18–19).'[4] The later use of the concept of immortality posed in relation to the question of survival (whether we survive or not) shifts this question to the quality of survival in its final outcome (the condition for survival), since it establishes a consequent necessity for affirming judgment on the wicked, now admitted to be also ontologically imperishable.

Obviously, immortality in the Hellenic sense differs from the preservation of the life of the righteous found in the biblical tradition. In essence, this tradition associated life after death closely with God's commitment to the life of the righteous. For these, their confidence in God's faithfulness initially generates the expectation that their life will be protected when faced with their enemies and threats of death. But evidence shows them that the violence of the wicked kills the righteous and their people. So this expectation gives way to hope of survival after death. But this is a hope that is not passive, since it is founded precisely on the faithfulness *of* God and on faithfulness *to* God. For this reason it is a hope that becomes strength for the

Resurrection as Process of a New Life

righteous to resist and to commit themselves to doing justice. How the survival of the righteous comes about is not clear. While survival through memory is affirmed, it seems to follow that the righteous survive in God's memory.[5] But the integral view of human beings as bodily and spiritual brings hope of equally integral survival and establishes survival after death as re-constitution of the whole person.

The experience of Israel enables us to glean some important anthropological traces for situating resurrection. The question of survival is tied in with the expectation of God's faithfulness in protecting his faithful from unjust death. Resurrection comes to be seen as a hope that has direct implications for practices of resistance and faithfulness.

II. They had no fear: the encounter with God's faithfulness

With respect for the weightiness of the subject, this received tradition of the Israelite experience of faith is found clearly expressed in the New Testament as the affirmation of God's infinite love, which covers all human needs and does not abandon human beings even at the hour of their death. The 'miracle' (*semeion*, sign) accounts of the resurrection in the Gospels generally and fundamentally carry this message: God's merciful love comes to offer life in the face of obvious threats of death. The context of faith in the resurrection also consists here clearly of the faithfulness of God, in whom absolute trust can be placed. In this sense, Jesus' resurrection is presented as the supreme proof of this faithfulness on God's part, since it is God's own Son who submits to the experience of unjust death, maintaining his trust in God's justice. Peter's sermon (Acts 2.14–35) at Pentecost argues in this direction, as I have already indicated. Jesus went through life doing good; he was unjustly put to death, but he overcame death, since he now lives. In other words, Jesus' experience of passing through death and rising again is the response and means to a solution to the great human question of survival in the face of death and of the violence that kills.

Following our concern to analyze the moral dimension of resurrection, it should be noted that Jesus' experience becomes a sign calling for human participation in this, his means to solving the challenge of survival. The implication of this is to stress the summoning power of Jesus' resurrection and to place resurrection in general in the context of discipleship. Trust in God's faithfulness, encouraged by signs and by the greatest sign shown in Jesus, opens up the way to commitment to God's justice, notwithstanding the unjust and death-dealing violence evident in the processes of history. Disciples are called to learn the way of resurrection.

III. Learning to raise and to act

The raising of Lazarus in John's Gospel (11.1–54) seems to be an anthological setting for perceiving the steps in discipleship in this regard. The commentaries by J. Mateos and J. Barretto on this passage include some steps on the road to resurrection:

(a) The first challenge to the community (vv. 1–17) is to overcome the *fear of death* and, consequently, *fear of the hostility* of the world: 'Jesus does not eliminate physical death; but for those who receive life from him, death is no more than sleep.'[6]

(b) Next (vv. 18–27), the community is called to place life and death in a wider context: 'God's creative project is to make human beings destined not for death but for full and definitive life, communicating God's own life to them. Such is the Father's plan and Jesus' messianic work. In this way the last and definitive stage of creation is inaugurated.'[7]

(c) The experience of death is painful (vv. 28–38a) and therefore demands compassion and solidarity.

(d) But the announcement of definitive life is at hand (vv. 38b–46) through the vigorous call to come out from the conditions of death. The challenge to the disciples is 'to trust in his word, to take the stone away, and to loosen the bonds of the old conceptions of death, which oppressed human beings, reducing their destiny to the condition of corpses. Death as the end of life is the high point of human frailty, which casts its net over all other frailties and humiliations. Fear of death as ultimate disappearance renders us powerless against oppression and upholds the power of oppressors. By freeing them from this basic fear, Jesus sets us radically free. Human beings cannot be ready to give their lives like Jesus if they are not convinced that they are indestructible. Only the certainty of possessing themselves fully beyond death frees their capacity for generous and total self-giving'[8]

(e) Realism shows that full and definitive life comes about in the midst of conflicts with the dominant power, which brings death (vv. 47–53): 'The Judaic power structure identifies the survival of the nation with its own. In this way, it justifies its political opportunism and the injustice it commits.'[9]

IV. Resurrection as encounter with gratuitousness

Resurrection is situated, as shown above, within the wider context of creation, in which human beings themselves share. This would seem to be extremely illuminating for understanding it as response to the question of human survival. This is seen in terms of everyday concerns and requires food, shelter, and endless other factors to sustain it. And notwithstanding human efforts to secure one's survival, death is an inevitable reality. A common path taken by human beings to ensure their life in the midst of this precariousness is to use violent force to exploit the resources for life in their environment. To this end, they will not stop at killing.

Jesus points to another path in his teaching and actions: 'For those who want to save their life will lose it, and those who lose their life for my sake will find it' (Matt. 16.25; cf. 10.39; Mark 8.35; Luke 9.24; 14.26; 17.33; John 12.25; 15.13). The course of life this implies is radical, since it shifts the axis from concern for one's own survival to focus it on concern for the survival of all. In this way, resurrection is situated in confrontation with a mentality centred on one's own interests. And it is presented as conversion (*metanoia*) to the mentality of the good news, which leads to sharing resources and one's own life. Conversion is a process on the way to encounter with gratuitousness. This process entails an experience of death understood as *self-denial*. This is at the same time the experience of shared life.

The novelty of Jesus' proposal does not reside simply in an ethical social solution to the problem of survival – overcoming violence and introducing sharing, that is. The surprising novelty lies in showing that survival is a problem because life is not fully created. This is made especially clear in John's Gospel, where two phrases have become emblematic: 'I came that they may have life, and have it abundantly' (10.10), and 'I am the way, the truth, and the life' (14.6). To carry life to its fullness, the way is to learn gratuitousness from Jesus. The way of concentrating on one's own interests is treacherous and will not lead to full life (cf. Deut. 30.15–20). In this manner, resurrection is not simply a survival mechanism, nor even a response to refusal to accept unjust death. Resurrection is encounter with full life, in a process of creation that leads to its own undoing. Resurrection comes to show that the solution to survival does not lie in simply living on but requires transformation.

V. Living as risen beings as adherence to resurrection

A summary of Pauline theology on resurrection will certainly be catered for in other approaches beyond the scope of this essay. In fact, both the specific problems Paul tackles and the concepts with which he develops his reflection involve complexities not capable of being expressed in a few pages.[10] Here are just a few notes that may contribute to my subject.

Noteworthy, particularly in the Letter to the Colossians (2.12; also in Rom. 6.4), is the association Paul makes between Jesus' resurrection and Christian baptism. As José Comblin has noted, his reference to baptism as the experience of *being buried* and *raised* with Christ refers to the process of change of mentality and sharing in the new life of Christ. He emphasizes faith as condition and action of the Spirit to bring about the process of transformation of life.[11] Baptism, at the same time as being a sign of human choice, is also a sacramental sign of a greater process of creation, in which God acts with human participation. For Paul, the actual resurrection of Jesus is an act of God.[12]

The new life implied in this process comes about as the creation of a moral personality, which expresses itself in new attitudes and actions until it reaches a final completion. 'So if you have been raised with Christ, seek the things that are above, where Christ is seated at the right hand of God. [. . .] When Christ who is your life is revealed, then you also will be revealed with him in glory' (Col. 3.1, 4). This Pauline parenesis on the one hand emphasizes moral attitudes as stemming from the condition of being raised; on the other, it supposes that our actions confirm our adhesion to the process of resurrection, which will be revealed in God's time. If this were not the case, his exhortation would be useless. The whole process of resurrection is God's transforming work, but it depends on human participation.

VI. Resurrection as building definitiveness

Current theological endeavour is converging on understanding resurrection as a process. 'The resurrection of the flesh is inserted into a *process of resurrection* [. . .] and cannot be reduced to a moment in time. [. . .] The resurrection of the dead, precisely because it is eschatology, is a horizon that draws together future, present, and past and *raises those who are still to die.*'[13] In very general terms, but valuable for its moral reach, one biblical dictionary gives the succinct definition: 'to rise again is to discover, beyond death, a life of a new kind, consisting of new relationships among human beings and between them and God'.[14]

Within this general picture, the concept of *resurrection* involves innumerable approximations that seek to respond to specific questions, such as the meaning of life after death, corporeality after time and space, God's faithfulness to those unjustly killed. These and other similar questions have polarized treatises on the subject down the ages. The term can be reserved to references to the end of the process, emphasizing the after-death, or it can simply be taken to cover the whole process. Besides this, it can concentrate on understanding Jesus' resurrection or can deal with questions on our own resurrection.

It is worth remarking that, even in reference to Jesus, resurrection carries a moral connotation, as is already implied in situating resurrection within the following of the Master. Karl Rahner suggested that the course followed by Jesus leads to an encounter with life in its definitive form: 'the resurrection does not mean the start of a new period in Jesus' life, set apart as something new, but the continuation of the order of time. It is rather precisely the permanent and saved definitiveness of the one life of Jesus, who, by means of the death he faced in freedom and obedience, attained this permanent definitiveness of his life.'[15] Note the ethical dimension contained in 'by means of the death he faced in freedom and obedience'. Rahner understands resurrection as 'definitiveness', beyond time, but that he sees it as a process also seems clear from his statement that Jesus' resurrection experience is open to us in *faith in his resurrection* and at the same time in *hope of our own resurrection*, and that examination of Jesus' resurrection allows us to interpret the object of this hope of ours.[16]

In this sense we can say that 'Jesus' resurrection is intended to be this utopia brought about in our own world. Because resurrection means the eschatologization of the human reality, our introduction body and soul into the kingdom of God, the complete fulfilment of all the capabilities God has placed in human existence. With this came the annihilation of all the alienating elements that tormented life, such as death, pain, hatred, and sin.'[17]

Brought into the day-by-day historical process, the experience of our resurrection, seen in the mirror of faith in Jesus' resurrection, can be identified in glimmers and snippets that reveal the greater dynamism by which our life is guided in the direction of its definitive dimension. Leonardo Boff writes from the heart on this point: 'Resurrection is happening; it is an ongoing process. One heart opening out to another in love and forgiveness? Resurrection is happening there! People building more just and fraternal relationships? Resurrection is coming about there! Has some growth in life, especially that of the oppressed and condemned, come to pass? Resurrection is revealed in that! Someone has died a death as good as their life, perhaps one of sacrifice for the sake of their brothers and sisters? Resurrection has been fully begun there!'[18]

A brief summary by way of conclusion. Concern for survival is an ongoing preoccupation of human beings. This is why various attempts to find a solution are also continuing. Death, though, shows itself to be inexorable in biological processes. And it breaks out with insane violence in exploitation and killing in vain attempts to guarantee life. God's surprising solution leads humankind down another path. It shows, in Jesus, that creation is still not finished. In its final stage, in order to live we need to lose our fear of death and share the resources and processes of our life with others. The encounter with gratuitousness then becomes the long road towards life's final stage. This final stage can be called resurrection. At every little step we take towards gratuitousness, resurrection beats in us like the heart of God.

Translated by Paul Burns

Notes

1. I am grateful to Prof. Rafael Rodrigues de Silva for his suggestions, and to Rogério Gomes, post-graduate student, for the bibliographical contributions.
2. Ps. 16.10, recalled by Peter at Pentecost (Acts 2.27: 'let your Holy One experience corruption').
3. D. Sávio da Silva, 1999, *Habacuc e a resistência dos pobres: tradução crítica do profeta Habacuc*, Aparecida: Santuário, p. 311. In this valuable work, the author differs from the translations of J. Jeremias and E. Otto in the overall interpretation of the text and translation of this prophet.
4. 2002, *Jerusalem Bible*, Port. trans., São Paulo: Paulus, Intro. to Wisdom of Solomon, pp. 861–2.
5. In this context it is interesting to read Peter's sermon (Acts 2.29–35), in which David's living on is associated with God's faithfulness in guaranteeing him the Messiah as a descendant.
6. J. Mateos and J. Barretto, 1989, *O Evangelho de São João: análise lingüística e comentário exegético*, São Paulo: Paulinas, p. 472 (Port. trans of, 1982, *El evangelio de Juan – análisis lingüístico y comentario exegético*, Madrid: Cristianidad).
7. *Ibid.*, p. 479.
8. *Ibid*, p. 491.
9. *Ibid.*, p. 497.

10. See, e.g., J. D. G. Dunn, 1998, *The Theology of Paul the Apostle*, Grand Rapids: Eerdmans; Edinburgh: T. & T. Clark.
11. J. Comblin, 1986, *Epístola aos Colossenses e Epístola a Filêmon*, Petrópolis: Vozes; São Bernardo do Campo: Imprensa Metodista, pp. 57ff.
12. Dunn, *op. cit.*, here Port. trans. 2003, *A teologia do Apóstolo Paulo*, São Paulo: Paulus, pp. 280–3.
13. L. C. Susin, 'Ressurreição da carne: "Face-a-face": Brevilóquio sobre escatología e criação (II)', *Cadernos da ESTEF*, 1993, no. 11, p. 15.
14. L. Mouloubou and F. M. Dubuit, 'Ressurreição da carne', in *idem.*, ²2003, *Dicionário Bíblico Universal*, Aparecida: Santuário; Petrópolis: Vozes, p. 681 (Port. trans. of *Dictionnaire biblique universel*, Paris: Desclée, 1984).
15. K. Rahner, 1977, *Grundkursus des Glaubens*, Freiburg: Herder, p. 262.
16. *Ibid.*, p. 269.
17. L. Boff, *Jesus Cristo Libertador*, Petrópolis: Vozes, p. 99.
18. L. Boff, 'Via Sacra de Ressurreição', in *idem*, 1991, *Seleção de textos Espirituais*, Petrópolis:Vozes, p. 75.

The Resurrection of One Crucified: Hope and a Way of Living

JON SOBRINO

I. Dead and victims

Human beings understand death and what comes after it in a variety of ways. And this understanding can also shape their lives.

At times they have understood death as the ending of their existence in peace and with a degree of naturalness, and so, in cultures where the nation was considered more important than the individual, as in ancient Israel, they could say 'he reached the end of his years and went to be united with his ancestors'. At times, as with Christianity, life and fullness are posited after death: 'Happy those who die in the Lord'.

Overall, though, death remains a negative thing. Many feel the rift of separation with no consolation or resist accepting nothing (Unamuno). Epicurus can bring psychology some comfort: 'While you are alive you need not worry, and when you are dead you cannot worry'. Or, more solemnly, Socrates before his judges: 'Now is the time for us to part, me to death and you to life. Which is better? That is hidden from mortals. Only the divinity knows it.'

Today, in prosperous societies, although death is still resisted, there is an increasing tendency not to take death too seriously. It is hushed up, made up.

These, and many others, are reactions, if I may say so, to the death of the 'dead'.

There are, however, other deaths that carry with them an added element of scandal that cannot be grasped by reason or by faith. A major scandal is the death of children who have not lived out their days and who have even, in their innocence, been murdered. Ivan Karamazov found no consolation in the idea that children torn to pieces by dogs on the orders of a lieutenant could go to a place in which they would be integrated into a universal harmony: 'If they invite me to that heaven, from now on I'll send the invitation back'. This is the scandal that has no resolution, and it goes on happening. Children, and also adult and old men and women, are wickedly murdered by National Security regimes, or die as 'collateral damage', or as a result of perfectly avoidable hunger.[1] This why from now on we should take the commemoration of the 'Holy Innocents' seriously and not trivialize it as a piece of Christmas decoration.

Another scandal is the death by assassination of those who have worked and struggled for justice: from the prophets of Israel to the innumerable martyrs and fallen of the last thirty years in Latin America. It may be some comfort to know that their deaths have produced life, and that some of them go on living in some form. But the death of 'victims' remains a scandal: the best, those who defend the oppressed, are done to death by injustice.

All this is well known, but I repeat it here so as to provide a proper context for the body of this article. In the Christian tradition the fate of human beings is understood in the light of the fate of Jesus. What we need to be clear about is that Jesus did not end his life 'in the fullness of days' but as a 'victim',[2] and that his resurrection did not consist in giving life back to a corpse but in giving justice back to a victim. The central affirmation is then that 'the risen one is the crucified one', which is what John's Jesus also insisted on, by appearing as risen displaying his wounds.

This, which is so clear in the New Testament, has not usually been seen as such. And as a result, neither has it been usual to situate Jesus' death in relation to the crucified reality of the victims of history. A blindness, partly culpable, tends to descend over both things. That is what I am trying to overcome in order to understand both Jesus' resurrection and its meaning for today.

I shall go on to reflect on two things: one, more specific, the hope of the victims; the other, more general, Christian existence, here and now in history, in the light of the resurrection: a life in community with the crucified, in order to take them down from the cross, living already as risen, and walking – with humility in the face of the scandal of history – with the God of the poor and the victims. But first a final observation.

I am writing from a place of victims and I am trying to reflect from their situation, as an irreplaceable hermeneutical tool for understanding the texts that speak of a crucified man raised.[3] But the difficulty is obvious. The present writer and readers are not victims in the sense that the vast majorities of the poor and oppressed of history are. We have no primary experience of what they feel, suffer, and hope. The fact is that 'taking life for granted', our situation, is not at all the same thing as 'not taking life for granted', theirs. This does not mean that we can understand nothing of their situation, but neither can we presume that, from ours, we can deploy adequate concepts to understand it. And this, in my view, is a basic problem for a theology whose God is, precisely, a God of poor and victims – a problem that becomes unavoidable when speaking of death and resurrection. Therefore it is only riskily and tentatively that we can speak of what the resurrection of Jesus means for them. And, from their situation, we can perhaps speak of our hope.

II. A drama in two acts

Jesus' fate as death and resurrection was soon *universalized*. Proclaiming the fact of his *death* was important for avoiding docetism, but it brought the risk of putting the fact that he *was put to death* in the shade. Hope in his resurrection was also widespread, but the nature of the event brought the danger of stressing, unilaterally, God's *power*, putting God's *justice* in the shade. To avoid these dangers, let us recall the first Christian preaching on the resurrection, even if this has come down to us in stereotyped and already theologized form.

Jesus' resurrection was preached as a drama in two acts: '[This man] . . . you crucified and killed by the hands of those outside the law. But God raised him up, having freed him from death . . .' (Acts 2.23–4; cf. the same pattern in Acts 3.13–15; 4.10; 5.30; 10.39; 13.28ff). The raising of Jesus is, then, presented as a *response* by God to the unjust and criminal actions of human beings, as is expressed by the 'but'. And as it is a response, we need to be conscious of why Jesus was crucified if we are to understand it properly. Not just anyone was resurrected, but Jesus of Nazareth, who proclaimed the kingdom of God to the poor and defended them, who denounced and unmasked oppressors, and who was persecuted by them, condemned to death and executed, and who throughout all this kept his trust in a God who is Father and his openness to the will of a Father who always showed himself as God, ineffable, un-manipulatable. The conclusion the first Christians very soon drew was that Jesus was persecuted and executed *like the prophets* (1 Thess. 2.15). They also proclaimed him 'the holy one', 'the just one', 'the giver of life', with which the 'verisimilitude' of a final fullness is increased, but so is the scandal: that the world eliminates its best.

Resurrection, therefore, means first and foremost *doing justice to a victim*, not merely *giving new life to a corpse*, even if this is its logical presupposition. It refers not simply to a death, but to a cross; not simply to dead people, but to victims; not simply to a power, but to a justice.

III. The hope of the victims

Several important considerations follow from the resurrection of a crucified man. I begin my analysis with what strikes me as most fundamental: it introduces *hope* into history, into human beings, into the collective consciousness, as a sort of historical life-experience capable of giving shape to everything. But let us not be hasty: specifically, it is a matter of a *hope for the victims*. And by *victims* here I mean both the great masses of the poor and oppressed who are put to death slowly and those who are assassinated for denouncing injustice and actively seeking justice.

It is true that the resurrection can be, and has been, used to release hope in a life 'beyond' for everyone. But if the person resurrected is a victim, the hope it produces is hope precisely for victims; they can hope for the justice and life that have been denied them in a thousand ways. In the well-known words of Max Horkheimer, speaking in the fullness of his years, we can hope 'that the executioner may not triumph over the victim'.[4]

This is the plot of the second act of the drama: God raised Jesus, and since then there is hope for the victims. But we need to define this carefully, or the conclusion can seem excessively *literalistic* as to the content and excessively *daring* as to the means of coming to express it.

It is not literalistic, however, since it is in line with the hope produced in Israel since the beginning, expressed in faith in a God who was constitutionally on the side of the victims. This is made clear in Exodus. In the Prophets, in order to judge oppressors harshly, God apostrophizes them as 'you', a distancing term that is followed by other threats, while he calls the oppressed 'my people' (Isaiah, Amos). Jesus, following in the same vein, proclaims the coming of the kingdom uniquely to the poor, as Joachim Jeremias says, telling them specifically that they will 'be filled' and 'laugh' (Luke 6.21ff): not so the rich, who will 'be hungry' and 'mourn and weep' (6.25). This partiality of God's very nature and of his promises, full of compassion and justice, shines out with absolute clarity from the resurrection of Jesus.

The second objection needs to be taken more seriously: the daring in speaking of the hope *of the victims*, as I have suggested – especially when by *victims* are understood not only individuals who freely decide to fight for justice but also the poor and oppressed majorities. The 'others', these poor, introduce an asymmetry (Levinas) into reality, which cannot be compensated in concept. The conclusion from this is that we non-poor cannot know with any precision what hope in general, or the more specific hope in relation to death, means for today's victims. Neither do I know if Adorno's lucid (and

Christian) statement, 'Hope applies only to others, never to oneself', can be applied equally to poor and non-poor.[5] I do not actually believe that this can be applied to the poor. I rather see them as having full right to hope for themselves – and let us hope they also have hope for the rest of us.

This does not prevent us from being able to say something about what, faced with Jesus' resurrection, the victims think and feel as the great 'other' for us: the poor. But, again, let us not be hasty. It is often supposed that it is easy for them to have hope in another life beyond death, because life here is hugely hostile to them, which, according to Marx, would be the condition for making religion possible, and of which the religions took advantage in order to instil fear. But things are not so simple. I am going to quote not authors but a poor woman, who possessed almost nothing and whose sons had been vilely murdered: 'A life after death, without sufferings? How splendid!' I do not think she meant, 'There will finally be fulfilment' (alluding to Jesus' resurrection, about which she does not understand much), but, 'That will be an end to the suffering I have always undergone' (which she does understand, and so she finds the thought of such a future consoling).

I do not think it is possible for us to delve into the depths of the victims. It is easy to get to learn their specific hopes, but what their *overall hope, in its fullness*, is remains their secret. From the outside, I believe they can find hope in the resurrection of Jesus, who was crucified like them, but not when it is preached as mere 'doctrine', only when it is proclaimed as 'good news', accompanied by the love and credibility of an Archbishop Romero.

IV. The hope of non-victims

So what of the hope of the non-poor, the non-victims? I believe Jesus' resurrection can indeed generate hope for them, for us. But on two conditions.

The first has to do with the *actual reality* of the non-victims.[6] The condition is that they participate, even if only analogously, in the reality of the victims, so that their death is, in some way, like that of Jesus, on a cross. I hope the following will serve to illustrate this analogy. When one's own death is not just the product of physical limitations or the wear and tear of looking after oneself, but when it is the outcome of loving dedication to others and to the weakness, poverty, defencelessness of these others as a result of injustice, then there is a likeness between one's own life and death and Jesus' life and death. Then, and from a Christian point of view only then, one can also share in the hope of resurrection. In short, community in the life and fate of Jesus is what gives us hope of what was produced in Jesus being produced in us.

Outside this communion with the crucified – Jesus and the victims – however analogous it may be, resurrection only spells out hope of life after death. And according to the most classical doctrine, this possibility does not necessarily generate hope, since it can bring salvation or condemnation. For resurrection to be salvation, the condition is to 'die in a state of grace'. For it to generate hope, the condition is 'to die on the cross', reproducing – to a greater or lesser extent, of course – the life, mission, and fate of Jesus, in trust and availability to a God-Father to the end.

The second has to do with our *subjectivity*: How is it possible to overcome the scandal of death, which seems to put an end to all hope, whether we are poor or non-poor? The response is inescapably personal. But we can suggest a way: to face up to the greater scandal of the injustice that *already* brings death to the *victims* and try to conquer it through our life-choices.

The first condition means that the resurrection of a crucified person should challenge us not only with how we approach not only *our own future death*, but also with how we, in the here and now, approach *the death and life of others*. The second is the question of what we ourselves can do to give the victims hope.

With regard to the first condition applied to the non-poor, the evangelical precept of forgetting oneself to regain oneself – losing one's life to save it – is still valid. Those for whom their own death is the greatest scandal and their hope in an afterlife their main preoccupation will not have a Christian hope or one stemming from Jesus' resurrection.

And with regard to the second, forgetting oneself has to go hand-in-hand with remembering the victims, which leads to losing one's life for them, doing the opposite of what the victim-makers do. A determined, persevering struggle on behalf of the victims will not produce hope in us mechanically, but it can produce it. It is true that whenever there is true love, hope springs up. 'Not all life is an occasion of hope', says Moltmann, 'but the life of Jesus, who took the cross upon himself out of love, is.' Wherever there is love, the poor can have hope, and we can have it with them.

V. Living in accordance with Jesus' resurrection

Jesus' resurrection is discussed in various contexts in the New Testament. Up to this point I have concentrated on *hope*, which can well serve as a judgment around which what it means to be human revolves – which is rather, I think, what Bloch meant in *The Hope Principle*. Let me now add, briefly, other aspects surrounding Jesus' resurrection, which can, together with hope, mould a way of living as human beings and as Christians.

'The wounds of the exalted one': living as though already risen in history

In the resurrection, Jesus is exalted. He lives in fullness, but he keeps his wounds. Taking this the other way round, we might say that we live in the wounds of history, but we can also share in fullness. So let us now see how we can live as risen beings in history.

The concept is not new. The Christians of Corinth, surrounded by extraordinary signs, miracles, gifts of tongues, ecstasies, thought they were already living in the resurrection – and they did not even believe in the final resurrection. They came to curse Jesus, and Paul had to rebuke them: 'No one speaking by the Spirit ever says "Let Jesus be cursed"' (1 Cor. 12.3). Another somewhat closer example: in seminaries and convents the superiority of celibacy over other ways of life used to be justified on the grounds that it allowed a present sharing in the fullness of resurrection, by distancing us from the material conditions of existence and bringing us closer to celestial ones.

The idea is mistaken and dangerous but not totally crazy, since it would be absurd for Jesus to live in fullness and for nothing of this to be reflected back on us. The important thing is to know how we can already live as risen beings and under what conditions. I believe that, for this to come about, we need to live in history something of 'fullness' and of 'triumph', something that savours of an impossibility become real. Fullness always consists in love, and triumph in overcoming egoism. Let us look at this in three ways.

The first is a life in *freedom that overcomes self-centredness*. Freedom expresses 'fullness' when it introduces us into history in order to 'love', and it expresses 'triumph' when 'nothing is an obstacle' to it. Freedom is then – paradoxically put – binding oneself to history in order to save it. This is what, speaking of himself, as a victim, John's Jesus says: 'No one takes [my life] from me, but I lay it down of my own accord' (John 10.18). This is the freedom with which an Archbishop Romero lived: he loved the poor and loved nothing more than them (fullness); he allowed no fear to hold him back from any risk (triumph).

The second is the *joy that overcomes sadness*. In situations of great suffering it may seem stupid to speak of joy, but it is possible, and even necessary, and it is found in communities of the poor. They come together to sing and celebrate, to express the joy of being together (fullness). And they can do this because, as Gustavo Gutiérrez once heard said in a community of poor people, 'The opposite of joy is not suffering but sadness. We suffer, but we are not sad' (triumph). In the midst of a thousand problems, Oscar Romero used to say, 'It's not hard to be a good shepherd to this people'.

The third is *the justice and love needed to 'take the crucified down from the cross'*. Here we are facing an extreme case of analogy: living as risen beings means living as beings who raise, 'take the victims down from the cross', 'give them new life'. This is what Bishop Pedro Casaldáliga proclaims in his contributions to this issue: 'Because I shall be raised, I must go about raising and provoking resurrection. Only those who lose their life will save it. . . . Every act of faith in resurrection has to have a corresponding act of justice, of service, of solidarity, of love.' Giving new life to the victims is fullness, and overcoming selfishness and the risks and fear it involves is triumph.

'The firstborn within a large family': in community with the victims

The first generation of Christians thought that Jesus' resurrection had brought the universal resurrection close (1 Thess. 4.15, 17; 1 Cor. 15.51). This did not happen, but the intuition was kept: Jesus did not rise alone, but as 'the firstborn within a large family' (cf. Rom. 8.29; 1 Cor. 15.3; Col. 1.18; Rev. 1.5). The resurrection implies communion of some with others, a logical presupposition in cultures in which individualism had not taken root: speaking of the 'fullness' of an isolated individual makes little sense.

If the firstborn is someone who has been crucified, we can well understand the eschatological community as above all a community of the poor and victims – as is already implied in the tradition of the Maccabees – and then, by extension and analogously, as the universal community. Specifically, we can understand the Church as the Church of the poor. From Latin America comes the statement that the poor are 'its principle of structuration, of organization, of mission'.[7] And Moltmann, for his part, insists that, ultimately, the true Church is present in 'the latent brotherhood of the universal judge hidden in the poor'.[8] Christian life is 'in community' and at its centre is the firstborn, 'a victim'. The poor and the victims are not only the recipients of the Church's ethical activity; they are its centre. They are the hinge that makes it operate in a Christian fashion.

'The firstborn in faith': walking humbly with God in history

Jesus is the firstborn in reaching God. But he is also the firstborn in journeying towards God. He walked in history doing justice and loving kindness, as Micah says. He is the firstborn in faith (Heb. 12.2). I end with a consideration of 'walking humbly with your God' (Micah 6.8).

I have already said how Jesus did this: he walked in trust in a God who is *Father* and in openness to a Father who is *God*. He walked *resting in* the Father and open to a God who *did not let him rest*. His resurrection was the ultimate encounter with this God Father.

We are on the way towards this same God, as mysterious for us as he was for Jesus. And the fact that the end of this journey is presented to us as 'resurrection' does not deprive the journey of mystery but heightens it. We can glimpse, hope, but we have to go on walking.

I believe the experience of the ultimate mystery always happens through particular experiences. Through the elements of which they are composed, they make us think without the mind or heart relaxing; they attract without us being able to reach what is always farther ahead of – or farther behind, or above, or below – us; they enlighten our sight without altogether dispersing the darkness; they gladden the heart without silencing Ivan Karamazov's protest.

This being so, I believe that both the reality called 'resurrection' and the reality called God are made, so to speak, of suitable 'material' for experiencing the mystery. 'Resurrection' speaks of life and death, of the grace of some and the sin of others, the whole wrapped in finality – and without being able to 'prove' anything. 'God' offers himself to us as source of all life and as destiny that draws everything to greater fullness of life – in the midst of an infinite silence. Both realities are mystery.

It is true that props are always provided: for the resurrection, the testimonies of the New Testament, the timing of the accounts, the honesty of the witnesses;[9] for God, the philosophical proofs of God's existence, reflection down the ages, the testimonies that, in the end, it is more possible to become fully human than without God. But I think that in both cases there is a disproportion and that 'the mystery remains a mystery'. I do not believe that a concept of God eliminates or reduces what is mysterious in resurrection or that a concept of resurrection eliminates or reduces what is mysterious about God. What happens is that both converge, mutually reinforce each other, and lead to an ultimate mystery: God all in all.

Perhaps we can formulate it in Micah's words. If we walk in history intending to bring the crucified down from the cross, showing kindness to the despised and silenced victims, if we walk humbly and in the silence demanded by the memory of Ivan Karamazov, we can perhaps, inwardly, allow the ultimate mystery, God, to mould our life. And perhaps we can have the hope that at the end of our journey we may meet with this God in the community of the risen. There can be no mere 'doctrine' to cover this. But we can make the experiment of hope being wiser than absurdity.

Translated by Paul Burns

Notes

1. '100,000 people die of hunger, or of its immediate consequences, every day. A child aged under ten dies every seven seconds, and every four minutes another goes blind from lack of Vitamin A. A child who dies of hunger today dies murdered.' Jean Ziegler, UN rapporteur for nutrition, interview in *El País*, 9 May 2005.
2. 'The statement that death is always the same proves as abstract as it is false': T. W. Adorno, 1975, *Dialéctica negativa*, Madrid, p. 371 (Eng. ed., 1973, *Negative Dialectics*, New York: Seabury).
3. I have developed this in, 1999, *La fe en Jesucristo. Ensayo desde las víctimas*, Madrid: Trotta (Eng. trans. 2001, *Christ the Liberator: A View from the Victims*, Maryknoll, NY: Orbis).
4. 1970 interview. The whole passage is splendid, still so today. It is especially illuminating on what theology is. 'The world is appearance, the world is not the absolute truth. Theology is the hope that this injustice that characterizes the world will not prevail for ever.'
5. 1995, *Gesammelte Schriften*, Frankfurt: Suhrkamp, pp. 34ff.
6. The term 'victim' is broad and complex. One can live in plenty and be victim of a dehumanizing system, to the extreme of slavery to drugs, for example. Here I am referring to human beings threatened in their basic life and dignity through oppression and repression.
7. I. Ellacuría, 'La Iglesia de los pobres, sacramento histórico de la liberación', in *ECA* 384–389 (Oct. – Nov. 1977), p. 717.
8. 1978, *La Iglesia, fuerza del Espíritu*, Salamanca, p. 160 (Sp. trans. of *Die Kirche im Kraft des Geistes*; Eng. ed., 1977, *The Church in the Power of the Spirit*, London: SCM Press).
9. To make it more acceptable, it is said that the Christian understanding of resurrection is more believable than others because it brings together the bodily, social, and even cosmic aspects of human beings: unlike, for example, the symbols derived from Greek philosophy.

Resurrection and Funeral Liturgy

ANDRÉS TORRES QUEIRUGA

Funeral ritual is as old as human history. Christianity engages with this human *continuum* but does so from its particular experience of the divine, in a definitive manner, based on its faith in the resurrection of Jesus the Christ. For this reason, the deep theological renewal taking place on this crucial point requires a corresponding renewal both in understanding of the innermost meaning of the Christian celebration of death and in the form taken by the rites. Vatican II laid down the basic principle: 'The rite for the burial of the dead should evidence more clearly the paschal character of Christian death' (SC 81).

Precisely because it is so important, however, and because it touches such deep spiritual chords, ancestral customs, theological and liturgical routines, and even economic constraints conspire to make the transformation problematic. Hence the importance of drawing out the full implications of the new theology of resurrection, since renewal has been such that, on the theoretical level, the principles have been laid down but the consequences have not always been drawn, while liturgical practice still preserves many remnants that made sense only from the earlier viewpoint. These are the basic lines followed in this reflection.

I. Christ, 'firstborn from the dead'

The traditional conceptualization was strongly marked by a 'miraculous' view of the resurrection, which tended to interpret it as 'bringing back to life'. Minds, as well as museums, were full of images in which the risen Christ could be seen, heard, and touched. This vision has been radically banished: we now understand the resurrection neither as miracle,[1] nor even as 'historical event' (real, but not accessible to historical investigation). Simply through his mysterious grandeur, from being introduced into the divine transcendence, the risen Christ is above the laws of time and space. Today not even serious theologians who assert the historicity of the *empty tomb* make *faith* in the resurrection depend on it, and as a result it would no longer be considered a 'proof' of the resurrection.[2] This means that there is an obvious logical inconsistency when this result is not applied to the *appearances*,[3] arguing that without these the resurrection would be reduced to a mere subjective illusion.

Such insistence supposes a false objectivism, falling into an 'empiricist trap', which theology should avoid with the greatest care, since, while seeming to defend faith, it is actually making it impossible. As Flew's parable of the 'invisible gardener',[4] designed to disprove the existence of God, shows, demanding *empirical* manifestations of a transcendent reality *a priori* annuls all possibility of proof. On the other hand, stating that 'no one shall see' God (Ex. 33.20) does not prevent, but guarantees, God's reality. 'Seeing' God would mean something empirical and finite: not God but an idol.[5] The same holds: denying the possibility of *empirical* appearances is the only way of guaranteeing the *authentic* reality of the risen Christ: you cannot 'see' someone capable of being present simultaneously in a Eucharist in Manhattan, Burundi, or Canberra; claiming to see him would be seeing not him but a phantasm, an imaginary creation. There is also one basic fact: Old Testament revelation shows that revelation of resurrection – *real*, not imaginary – happened without 'appearances' or 'empty tombs', but based instead on divine faithfulness, backed up by the experience of martyrdom (see Daniel and 2 Maccabees).

In reality, beyond possible quibbles over details, this understanding stems from irreversible currents in Christology: Jesus' divinity appears *in* his humanity. Rahner was right to insist on this: far from being opposed, the two reinforce each other: the more human, the more divine. Avoiding the 'miraculous' does not diminish the resurrection but frees it from the empiricism of mere 'bringing back to life'. Leaving aside the chronological literalism of 'the third day', the death of Christ is a true 'going to the Father', 'dying towards the inner reality of God'.[6] This is the Johannine *hýpsosis*: physical elevation on the cross and exaltation in God. The resurrection happens on the cross. Once empiricism is discarded, universality takes its place, in that identity-difference that defines our relationship with Christ: for us too dying is rising already.

The conciliar principle, 'only in the mystery of the incarnate Word does the mystery of man take on light' (GS 22a), is truly fulfilled here. In the present context, this is decisive and calls us still to make universality complete, leaving behind the *chronological* interpretation of the primacy of Christ – which reduces his resurrection to a mere temporal beginning– God did not rise before this – and relegates the general resurrection to the future – God will raise the dead only on the last day. This view seemed to project the greatness of Jesus and exalt divine action. In reality it isolated Jesus, estranging him from history and belittling God by making him, contrary to what Jesus himself said, the 'God of the living' only from the first century AD. On the other hand, an interpretation respectful of transcendence shows that Christ's resurrection *reveals in fullness* what God was doing with his children from the beginning of the world.

This interpretation, neglected in theology,[7] can seem strange at first, but it becomes understandable if we think of the divine fatherhood. No one before Jesus had spoken so fully of God as *Abbá*; but this does not mean that God began to be *Abbá* early in the first century: we understand rather that it was *then* revealed what God had been *for ever*. Equally, never before Christ had resurrection appeared in all its fullness – *already*, without waiting for the end of time, and *totally*, not a soul waiting for a body –; but neither does this imply that God has been raising the dead only for the past two thousand years.

Put as brutally briefly as that, this overall re-interpretation may seem strange.[8] But I believe that, once we escape from the enchantment of the traditional conceptualization, it is not difficult to see it as responding to the needs of our cultural situation and as verifying the conciliar principle: truly, the mystery of our resurrection is revealed in the resurrection of Christ.[9] Christ is 'the firstborn from the dead' (Col. 1.18), as he is 'the firstborn of all creation' (Col. 1.15); this, though, does not indicate 'a temporal priority but one in rank or dignity, of Lordship over all that exists'.[10]

II. The basic paradigm: Christ, 'firstborn from the deceased'

Such an understanding is decisive for understanding the liturgy for the dead, and I shall base my remarks on it. In fact, as the section heading shows, we need to take one further step, daring to translate as 'firstborn from the *deceased*'. Because words, like coins, wear out with age. Used as we are to hearing 'firstborn from the dead', we can miss the deep realism of the expression. Jesus *really* died: dead as one of the dead; nevertheless, we believe that he *really* lives: 'I was dead, and see, I am alive' (Rev. 1.18). He is truly deceased, since 'deceased' – as we definitively know thanks to him – means someone who died but who lives: he died to one stage, aspect, or dimension of his life but entered into the definitive life, identified with God.

It is worth insisting on this point, so as to draw the consequences. Let us imagine a priest coming to the altar and announcing, 'Dear brothers and sisters, we are gathered here to celebrate, in faith and hope, the death and resurrection of our deceased brother Jesus of Nazareth'. This would cause some surprise. Nevertheless, this is what the congregation quite naturally declares not much later: 'Christ has died; Christ is risen; Christ will come again'.

So, continuing in this realist vein, it now becomes more understandable to state that every Christian liturgy of the dead consists in 'celebrating the death and resurrection of our deceased brother/sister N/N'. The difference from Christ should not obscure the underlying identity, so stressed by St Paul: 'if the dead are not raised, then Christ has not been raised' (1 Cor. 15.16); nor should it erase the radical continuity: he is not only 'firstborn' but also 'first fruits' (*aparché*; 1 Cor. 15.20, 23).[11]

This is undoubtedly the core of the Mass for the dead. The light emanating from it shows up the truth of everything else or lays bare its falsity. In it we celebrate one of the great titles of God: the One who saves from death. This is why we glorify him and why we celebrate the rout of 'the last enemy' (1 Cor. 15.26). We learn it from Jesus and proclaim it for ourselves: 'Those who believe in me, even though they die, will live' (John 11.25). Take the 'raising' of Lazarus as an example: if we interpret this literally in our critical culture, not only is the story absurd, but it is no consolation in what it would teach: 'friends' would come back to life, but others would not share the same privilege. Taken as a symbol, though, it is a magnificent proclamation of the essential. Paraphrasing Crossan, we might say, 'Lazarus was never raised; Lazarus is always risen'.[12] *We are all Lazarus.*

The Eucharist affirms this faith, consolidates this hope, and should ensure its realism. Nothing is further from authentic Christian hope than thinking of the blessed as ethereal beings, depersonalized, with a diffuse identity, alien to the relationships and affections of their historical lives. Exactly the opposite happens: 'once I reach there, I shall be truly person (*ánthropos*)', Ignatius of Antioch magnificently said.[13] In this regard, Jesus' words, 'For in the resurrection they . . . are like angels in heaven' (Matt. 22.30), are often wrongly interpreted. These words, far from proclaiming a bloodless and depersonalized life, proclaim its ultimate fullness: love free from selfishness, without rivalry or exclusion, joy shared in infinite communion: 'we will be like [God]' (1 John 3.2).

This is the fruitful core from which we must order our understanding and define the consequences.

III. Celebrating 'with' the deceased, not 'for' the deceased

One decisive consequence clearly follows, but it demands the utmost clarity of language: we do not celebrate the Eucharist *for* our deceased sister/brother, *but* with them (just as we do not celebrate it *for* Jesus but *with* Jesus). The deceased person is no mere memory or passive object, deaf and blind to our presence. *Like Christ*, from God, though invisible to us, he/she is transfigured presence, total love.[14] Celebrating the death and resurrection of our deceased means *truly* being able to talk to talk to them, knowing they are listening; communing with them, knowing they love more than ever; living the same life as them, that of God in all.

As sacrament, furthermore, the Eucharist is the privileged act that unveils the universality of the presence: not an isolated parenthesis but revelation of true and ultimate reality: *from God, our dead-raised are always and everywhere with us*. It is not artificial to speak to them, to experience their presence, to rejoice in their happiness, to know ourselves wrapped in their love. In effect, this is what Christian piety has always done in its relationship with the canonized 'saints' – and all those who are with the Lord in glory are saints. Given the sobriety required in approaching these matters and the restraint in language they impose, we can still intuit how elevated and vital what is celebrated here really is. Some deformations are unmasked in the process, and many practices lose all legitimacy.

On this point, it is worth proposing a further and more realistic development of the precious dogma of the *communion of saints* (of all, not only those canonized). This reflects – in all its realism, specificity, and universality – the reality of eternal life as the founding root that, by making us all daughters and sons of God, establishes humankind as a true family, making dwelling together in fellowship, the 'new commandment' of love and service, the supreme norm. On the other hand, as I shall go on to say, we need to erase the false image of the saints as 'intercessors' before God, so as to see them as multiple mirrors that reflect, each in their own way, different aspects of the infinite divine mystery ('Since my sister died, I see God in another colour', a deeply sensitively devout friend of mine once said); and by the same token – as Von Balthasar rightly insists – also as openers of new doors for theology and Christian life. The authentic space of our life-experience is thereby organized, in both its directions: toward God (and the deceased) and toward ourselves.

IV. We have no need to 'convince' or to 'placate' God

What this changes radically is above all the nature of our prayer. The basic structure of the liturgy aims to celebrate the victory of God's love over death. There is no sense in trying to 'supplicate' God, and still less in trying to 'placate' God by imploring his mercy to the deceased. When we dwell on the infinite goodness of the 'God of life', who has done and goes on doing everything to rescue his children from death, it is amazing that we should be trying to 'convince' God, as if our love for the deceased were greater than God's or our concern for them deeper than God's. Of course no one is consciously intending this, but the *objective nature* of our Bidding Prayers and rituals too often *implies* that we are the good and merciful ones, that we are making the effort to influence and 'propitiate' a cruel, vengeful, and terrible god.[15]

A long tradition has led to the liturgy being full of prayers that, without lacking in great qualities, *in their literal expression* make God's mercy depend on our petitions, blotting out the glorious truth of God's pre-existing, gratuitous, and unconditional love. The burial rite is not lacking in formulas of respect and trust, but its most common prayer formula is: 'hear our prayers . . . and let our brother/sister'. The result is all too often shocking: 'Open your ears to the clamour of our supplications and may your eyes be moved to sorrow . . .'; 'have mercy . . . so that N. may not suffer punishment'; 'be not severe in your judgment', and so forth. Furthermore, we still have prayers that imply that it is God who sends death, reinforcing a view that, by attributing evil to God, today can seem unbearable and traumatizing:[16] 'whom you have just called from this life', 'although we cannot comprehend why you wished to deprive us so painfully of the presence of our brother . . .'.

Respect for literary tradition should not consist in sacralizing its letter but in recovering its spirit. What might not have surprised people in earlier times very often seems intolerable today. (Who, like Augustine, would now consign unbaptized infants to hell,[17] or who, like Thomas Aquinas, would think that contemplating the torments of the damned increases the joy of the just in their glory?[18]) Even more so because the *letter* of many prayers originated at a time of literalism in revelation, which tended to level out biblical texts, without taking account of time differences. The result is that ideas from the Old Testament can be adopted as valid, without the corrections that the God revealed in Jesus is requesting. This is what has happened with the famous text of 2 Maccabees 12.46: 'It is a holy and a wholesome thing to pray for the dead, so that they may be freed from their sins.' In the thoroughly ritualized period of the Second Temple, when express consciousness of resurrection was still in its infancy, these would have been understandable, and they even represented a magnificent advance. But after Jesus' *Abbá* and the fullness revealed in his resurrection, nothing obliges us to retain their literal sense (though I shall go on to say something of a possible interpretation).

The *pastoral consequences* of a false view are only too well and sadly known, above all in certain environments: salvation has its price, and classes and rivalries are kept up before God. Fortunately, the scandal of first-class and third-class funerals has virtually vanished, and the commercial view – so many Masses and responses, so much more certainty of salvation – is disappearing. But it does no harm to remember it: first, because those practices went in *strict parallel* to those views, which are thereby shown up in all their falsity; second, because such views cannot be presumed to be totally dead, since they continue deeply imbedded in the collective mindset and can also survive under renewed and subtle guises. Funerary establishments, for strictly commercial reasons, fight against the gratuitousness of salvation and seek to blur the absolute equality of the children of God. And a pastoral strategy that lacks the courage to renew itself from top to bottom, both in its preaching and in the re-structuring of its liturgy and the administration of stipends, can very easily lapse into deceit and continue the old routines under new forms.

V. Liturgy for our salvation

The above considerations have insisted on the exquisite care – never enough – needed in our speech about God, out of respect for God's infinite stature and goodness. They have also consistently been based on the ideal, on the authentic 'essence', that is, of celebration. The time has come to stress the reality, accepting the inevitable deficiencies of our constructs and the needy obscurity of our faith. Because the marvel of what we celebrate is here in its mystery, but we need to assimilate it, opening ourselves to the suffusion of its efficacy. We need to do this in three principal aspects.

Above all, celebrating the death of our deceased eucharistically means, of course, confessing our faith and experiencing our hope. But at the same time it means *nourishing that faith and grounding that hope*, because the terrible darkness of death continually wears down the certainty of resurrection, and the brutal realities of the material world put the innermost and problematic insights of faith to the test. The celebration of our dead – with the living recall of its symbolic expression and with the warmth of the community's life-experience – provides a permanent source of nourishment, a needed viaticum for the endless journey of strengthening faith and nourishing hope. (Whence, once again, the need to choose expressions with care and to decipher meanings correctly.)

Next comes the cultivation of *solidarity*. Celebrating together – as the various funerary rites have always known – provides the best way to accompany the sorrow of those most directly affected. First, on the most psychologically and immediately human level of physical proximity, through helping to assimilate the trauma that death always represents. And also, in the directly religious dimension, insofar as this proximity transcends and reinforces itself through common prayer, through the joint statement of our faith, and the celebration of our shared hope. Christian understanding proclaimed this from the earliest times: 'Therefore encourage one another with these words' (1 Thess. 4.18).

This solidarity should not be reduced to the moment of death or just the liturgical celebration; it should extend to the whole of everyday life. The *meditatio mortis* has always been a guiding light for genuineness of life, and it has become even more relevant in our days. This comes about in the existentially most intimate aspect of our lives. Heidegger poses the assumption of the *Sein zum Tode* as the condition for authenticity. For his part, Franz Rosenzweig begins his most important work with these words: 'All understanding of the All begins with death, with the fear of death'; he, though, unlike Heidegger, makes this lead out, most significantly, into words of life: 'Toward what do the leaves of this door open? Do you not know? Toward life.'[19] And this applies also in the social and historical aspects, as the concern for the victims in the political theology of liberation shows.[20]

In general, the celebration of death, with its reference to the ultimate values and the view of existence as bound up in the communion of saints and God's immeasurable and all-embracing love, undoubtedly provides religious sensibility with a special opportunity for setting a course for our personal lives and acting to remove the lack of caring, the hatreds and divisions that paralyze living together in community.

In this context, there is still a third, subtler and more mysterious, aspect: *this-worldly solidarity with the deceased*. I have already said that the movement of transformation should not be directed upwards, to 'convince' or 'placate' God, or even to 'alleviate' the deceased brother or sister, who are already welcomed and sheltered in the divine love and life. Transformation makes sense only toward 'below', toward this world, toward the renewal of our lives. In fact, without falling into magical supernaturalisms, *we can really help our deceased*, inasmuch as, for good or for evil, the influence of their lives and behaviour remains at work in persons and institutions, continues to be open to history and in some way also entrusted to our solidarity. An undertaking begun and left unfinished at their death can be a call for us to carry it on: this is the truly fleshly reality of the communion of saints, and it can form the best proof of our love for, thanks to, and union with them. In the same way too, unpaid debts, the harmful effects of wrong or simply incomplete actions, can require our collaboration: that we 'help' our deceased – now that they no longer intervene in the actuality of history – to pay their debts, resolve harm they may have done, and even obtain forgiveness from any they have offended.

This is a deep – and possible and legitimate – meaning of the statement from 2 Maccabees already quoted: the invitation to 'pray for the dead, so that they may be freed from their sins'. A literal view, which would be trying to obtain God's forgiveness on their behalf, offers every handle to Kant's furious critique in his justifiable protest against a 'satisfaction' that would remove the freedom of those concerned, without supposing an internal change in them.[21] The interpretation suggested here, on the other hand, preserves the moral integrity of the deceased, who are safe in the loving hands of God, while opening the effects of their historical presence to the solidarity of their brothers and sisters. In this way, the communion of saints completes its vertical sense, as it were, with a horizontal sense, which works as a blessing in the real life of the community.

Translated by Paul Burns

Notes

1. Well expressed in the title of the Italian translation (by L. Sudati) of a work of mine: 2006, *La risurrezione senza miracolo*, Molfeta (BA): La Meridiana.
2. In Catholic circles this is taken up in recent monographs, such as H. Kessler, [2]1987, *Sucht den Lebenden nicht bei den Toten*, Düsseldorf; Th. Lorenzen, 1995, *Resurrection and Discipleship*, Maryknoll, NY: Orbis; F. G. Brambilla, [2]1999, *Il Crocofiso risorto*, Brescia; M. Deneken, 1997, *La foi pascale*, Paris; E. Castellucci, *Davvero il Signore è risorto*, Assisi. Among Protestant scholars, W. Pannenberg himself, an energetic defender of the empty tomb, personally confirmed this interpretation to me: see 1991, *Systematische Theologie*, 2, Göttingen, pp. 395, 405.

3. It is noteworthy that J. D. G. Dunn distances himself from the most common view, considering the empty tomb more likely: 'It should be noted that I am reversing the common argument . . .', 2003, *Jesus Reconsidered*, Grand Rapids: Eerdmans; Cambridge, CUP, p. 840, n. 64.
4. A. Flew, 'Theology and Fabrication', in, 1951, *Essays in Logic and Language*, Oxford: Blackwell.
5. This is clearer still in N. R. Hanson, who would allow the existence of God only if he appeared as a vast thundering Jupiter, who could be caught on video and audio tape: see, 1971, *What I Do Not Believe and Other Essays*, New York: Humanities Press.
6. H. Küng, 1977, *On Being a Christian*, London: SCM Press (here Sp. trans, *Ser Cristiano*, Madrid, 1977, p. 455); cf. K. Rahner, 1976, *Grundkurz des Glaubens*, Freiburg, p. 262: 'in diese [die Auferstehung] hineinstirbt' ('he dies toward the resurrection'); also the considerations by Kessler, *op. cit.*, p. 300.
7. This is briefly but clearly stated by R. Haight, 1999, *Jesus, Symbol of God*, Maryknoll, NY: Orbis, p. 147.
8. I seek to supply a broad and detailed grounding in my, ^{3}2004, *Repensar la resurrección. La diferencia cristiana en la continuidad de las religiones y la cultura*, Madrid: Trotta (Galician original, Vigo, 2002).
9. It is worth pondering Karl Rahner's words: 'We posit the unicity (*Einmaligkeit*) of Jesus falsely when we view him solely as the Son of God who comes to meet certain people who from the start have nothing to do with God, when we see him simply as an emissary from a divine beyond to a world that has nothing to do with God. In reality, nevertheless, we are children of God in the whole history of humankind' ('Kirchliche Christologie zwischen Exegese und Dogmatik', in, 1970, *Schriften zur Theologie*, 9, p. 212).
10. L. F. Ladaria, 1983, *Antropología teológica*, Rome, p. 23; cf. pp. 17–26, where he analyzes other parallel texts: 1 Cor. 8.6; Heb. 1.2–3; John 1.3, 10.
11. This is stressed equally by J. D. Crossan,: 'Jesus and all other mortals are either exalted together or fall together' (1994, *Jesus: A Revolutionary Biography*, San Francisco: Harper, which synthesizes his major works), and J. D. G. Dunn: '[this metaphor] can have been coined only by those who did indeed regard Jesus' resurrection as the beginning of the (general) resurrection of (all) mankind (1 Cor. 15.21)' (*Jesus Reconsidered, op. cit.*, p. 869).
12. 'The road to Emmaus never existed. But we are always on the road to Emmaus' (*op. cit.*, p. 213).
13. *Letter to the Romans*, VI, 2.
14. This is a basic theme to which insufficient attention has been paid: cf. H. Urs von Balthasar, 1980, *Kennt uns Jesus – Kennen wir ihn?*, Freiburg; K. Rahner, 1982, *Was heist Jesus lieben?* Freiburg; *idem.*, 1991, *Wer ist dein Bruder?*, Freiburg. Our relationship with Christ stems from the gospel, but it cannot be physical as his disciples' was. But neither is it reduced to a mere memory, nor is

it less real. It obeys a sort of Kantian dialectic, in which memory enlightens presence (which would be blind without it) and presence fills memory (which would be empty without it). I have written on this in, ³2001, *Repensar la Cristología*, Estella, pp. 291–8, and *Repensar la resurrección, op. cit.*, pp. 285–92.
15. This, which holds for prayer in general (see my 'Beyond Prayer of Petition', *Concilium* 2006/1, pp. 63–75), takes on a special relevance here.
16. Allow me to indicate my, 2000, *Del Terror de Isaac al Abbá de Jesús*, Estella; and 'La inevitable y posible teodicea' in *Iglesia Viva* 225 (2006), pp. 9–30.
17. In effect, the Council expressly indicates that, 'The rite for the burial of infants is to be revised, and a special Mass for the occasion provided' (SC 82).
18. *STh Suppl.*.q. 94, a. 1–3; cf. q. 99, a. 1, ad 4; also St Gregory the Great, *IV Dialog.* ch. 44 (ML 77, p. 404).
19. F. Rosenzweig, ³1990, *Der Stern der Erlösung*, Frankfurt, pp. 3, 472.
20. On the subject of 'victims' see, *inter alia*, J. B. Metz (ed.), 1996, *El clamor de la tierra*, Estella; 1996, *Hope against Hope: Johann Baptist Metz and Elie Wiesel Speak Out on the Holocaust*, New York; J. Sobrino, 2003, *Christ the Liberator: An Essay from the Victims*, Maryknoll, NY: Orbis.
21. Cf. e.g., 'Since by the said deduction we can see that an absolution before the heavenly justice for man laden with guilt can only be thought of under the supposition of a complete change of heart, it follows that all expiations, whether of a penitential nature or of a solemn nature, all invocations and glorifications (including that of the atoning ideal of the Son of God) cannot make up for the absence of such a change, or, if this is present, cannot augment, even in the slightest, its validity before that tribunal' (1793, *Die religion innerhalb der Grenzen des blösen Vernunft,* here trans. from Sp. trans, 1969. p. 79; Eng. trans., ²1960, by T. Meyer Greene and H. H. Hudson, *Religion Within the Limits of Reason Alone*, Chicago and New York: Open Court and Harper & Row).

I Believe in Resurrection

PEDRO CASALDÁLIGA

I respect all the faiths that try to explain and accept death, in their own way, but I believe in resurrection.

From my Christian faith this is the alternative: living or raised – living here as mortals, living 'there' as risen.

I am unable to conceive, hope for, welcome death – mine and that of all mortal people who journey through this land of Time – other than in terms of resurrection.

For my faith (with my theology) the dead do not exist. They passed through death and rose; we shall pass through death and we shall be resurrection, fullness of life in the mysterious realm of the fullness of God. All the dead are 'those dead who do not die', because they are raised (in that 'divine passive' of which biblical scholars speak).

Death, through which we 'pass' (all death is Passover), in innate in us, for sure. We are born to live, and this living, so beautiful and so precious, passes through death; we are children of clay, mortality walks with us like an enveloping shade. Resurrection is not innate in us: it is sheer free gift from the God of life.

Believing in resurrection does not make death any less 'the greatest of evils', as the Latin adage has it. All human fears come down, in the final analysis, to fear of death. Dying is always a matter of shadows, of severance, of existential trauma – a radical 'setting forth', the most radical of all, 'like a cliff from which we have to throw ourselves with our eyes shut', as the patriarch theologian José-María Díez-Alegría confided – though he immediately added, like the truly Christian confessor that he is, 'putting all our trust in God and saying to him, "You know better than I"', and walking 'with a joyful hope that I shall open my eyes'.

Miguel de Unamuno, that tragic prophet admirable in his so human rebelling, could not agree. 'If we die altogether', Don Miguel asked in anguish, 'What's it all for? For what? I don't want to die, no; I don't want to, nor do I want to want to; I want to live for ever and to live as me, this poor me who I am and feel myself to be here and now.' Nevertheless, with apologies to the Master of Salamanca, who now lives at peace in the full light, it is certain that 'we die altogether'; I am the one who dies, it's my person, not just my body; I am a unity in life and in death. Life is personal, death is personal, and . . . resurrection is personal. 'We die altogether and we rise altogether.' Christian personalism (even our God is a mystery of persons in fullness of relationship) can believe only in the death of persons and in the resurrection of the same persons. 'I myself shall see Him', protested that most upright old man, Job.

To cry out this faith, to strengthen myself in this hope, I repeat (to you and to myself) what I wrote in a sonnet titled just that: 'I myself shall see Him'. It goes like this:

> And we shall, for all time, be ourselves,
> as you are the One who, on our earth,
> was son of Mary and of Death,
> companion on all our journeys.
> We shall for ever be what we are
> but most gloriously restored,
> just as those five wounds you bore
> are indescribably glorious.
> As you are the One who, human, brother,
> was just the same as the One who died,
> Jesus, the like and the totally other,
> so shall we, exactly, for all time,
> be what we were and are and shall be,
> utterly other and yet ourselves quite.

This Christian faith of mine is a Passover faith, I stress; it is founded on and starts from the resurrection of Jesus of Nazareth, 'the firstborn from among the dead'. He is 'the Resurrection and the Life'. If Christ is risen, we too are risen: that is the certainty, plain and solid, of our Christian faith.

Now, my faith is as much personal as communitarian; I believe in Humankind, I believe in Church. If I am to be consistent with this personal-communitarian faith, I have to live hope in the resurrection making it credible for my neighbour, precisely here, today, in the vicissitudes of history, on this beloved, violent Earth of questions and lies and death.

The God of Resurrection is the God of Creation and the God of Redemption. We cannot vivisect the mystery of God, God's love incarnate in us and 'clothing' the whole of creation 'in his beauty'. No one can honestly profess faith in another, risen, life without professing truth, justice, and freedom in this life, during the disturbed time of our mortality. Faith in resurrection has to be political. If we are one day – that Day – to live the final gift of resurrection, we must live intrepidly in this everyday of history, risking this mortal life, which is also given to us by 'the Author of life'. Because I shall be raised, I must go about raising and provoking resurrection. Only those who lose their life will save it. 'On the other side' everything is down to God, and we can hope with confidence; on this side it is down to us, with the grace of God. To come to live the New Heaven and New Earth we have to go about renewing this heaven, so often veiled, and this earth, so despoiled. The worst service we can render faith in life-resurrection, which will be given to us, is to wash our hands irresponsibly of this life-militancy, which has been entrusted to us. Every act of faith in resurrection has to have a corresponding act of justice, of service, of solidarity, of love.

So I believe in resurrection. With the pithy slogan on many a wall in Our America, I passionately confess: 'It may cost us our lives, but we shall rise again'.

Translated by Paul Burns

Conclusion
Resurrection: the Heart of Life and Faith

LUIZ CARLOS SUSIN

In conclusion, gleaning and selecting something from all that has been argued, we can begin by stating what is most obvious: that the resurrection of the dead and, absolutely, the resurrection of Jesus, the crucified one who was raised – resurrection as *horizon* and as *event* – is the heart of human life and of the Christian faith: 'If there is no resurrection of the dead, then Christ has not been raised; and if Christ has not been raised, then our proclamation has been in vain and your faith has been in vain. . . . If for this life only we have hoped in Christ, we are of all people most to be pitied' (1 Cor. 15.13–14, 19).

Resurrection, as has been stated in several ways here, does not primarily have to do with establishing a firm basis for composing a doctrine or a religion. It has to do first and foremost with human life. And not with life in general, in the abstract, nor with a faint-hearted life or one dedicated to consumerism as if there were no more to hope for, as Paul nicely observes in relation to the suppressed despair of the proverb, 'Let us eat and drink, for tomorrow we die' (1 Cor. 15.32). On the contrary, life lived in joy and suffering, shared in compassion and in nonconformity – in the 'indiscipline' of the crucifixion protests, as Marcella Althaus-Reid says here –, life given and lost: this is the life that receives the 'good news' and bears fruits of resurrection. Therefore, resurrection is the heart of life, and it comes about in the heart of life just when death mortally wounds life. Our main concern to live comes before faith and hope, and it awakens faith and hope in resurrection, even if we give it other names. And, obviously, it comes before religion and teaching on life greater than death.

But is not faith in resurrection, in the end, faced with the reserve of the mystery of the beyond, as with the reserve of the mystery of creation and of the very God, merely a narcissistic desire springing from a mortal heart, like an ephemeral bubble fearful of vanishing with the first puff of wind? This is why, especially when we come to this heart of life, faith seeks to understand. The course followed by the various authors in this issue, an eminently theological course, is that of faith seeking to understand the resurrection of the dead.

The word *resurrection,* elevated to the dignity of central category in the profession of faith, finds it hard to support this weight of meaning. And, like all language, it can turn out to be laden with misunderstandings. Jon Sobrino, in the quest for the best expression of this mystery, took up, in his *Christ the Liberator,* Kant's famous basic questions concerning human beings: if resurrection is quite so decisive, even more so than this mortal life, 'What can we know? What must we do? What may we hope for?' Because resurrection becomes a fount of *knowledge,* of *praxis,* and of hope, in a circular dialectic. Here in less logical form, in order to recall and reflect for a final time on what has been said here, I am going to hang my remarks on three 'hooks': *language, experience, relationship.*

I. Language in respect of resurrection

Recalling Paul Ricoeur, perhaps we can state that the *resurrection of the dead* as horizon and the *resurrection of the crucified Jesus* as event neatly make up the Christian *myth par excellence.* Composed of metaphors, constructed from symbolic pieces, well-ordered 'mythologems' in narratives full of meaning, contextualized in a world suffering birth pangs, with recourse to tradition and renewal, syncretized with the most diverse narratives and cultural symbols throughout history and geographically (suffice to check the Andean example here), it is a great and beautiful myth, central to human existence.

In Ricoeur's words, the *myth* 'makes us think', since it deals in a language that introduces understanding and integration of experiences that in everyday life fade away into darkness or clash in mutual antagonisms. How do we, for example, think of the clamour for justice in a world where the executioner always triumphs over the victim? This is why Oscar Cullmann and Paul Tillich warned, each in his own way, that profession of faith in *resurrection* is not simply in *immortality,* nor is it simply derived from different cultural contexts.[2] The spiritual aristocracy of the Stoics, hovering above the realm of needs tied to the body, contented itself with the purity of immortality and despised preaching of the resurrection of the body. The bulk of the people, however, whose daily lives consisted in struggling physically, in suffering and rejoicing in their bodies, could not indulge in this Stoic luxury or dualist illusion. Resurrection, this word placed alongside so many other

Conclusion: Resurrection: the Heart of Life and Faith

metaphors, such as *lifting up, rapture, exaltation, glorification, justification*, and the whole poetics of narratives, dialogues, and actions established hope and faith centred on the body that suffers and dies, on human existence played out in mortality and bodily weakness. The profession of faith in respect of the resurrection of the dead became defined within the Church as resurrection of the *flesh*, precisely that dimension of corruptibility in which we live out our truly vital human experiences.

And so the great new myth, elaborated with the finesse and realism of the period, would be passed on down the ages. But the myth is, under another aspect, a 'ready-made' thought, like a ready-made garment, a thought *prêt à porter*: in homilies, in paintings, in the imagination. Simplified and dispensed in this way, it is also dangerous. Its danger lies precisely in its success: it dispenses us from thinking anew, from re-thinking. Because thinking, in the first instance, means bringing healing to the wounds of existence. Thinking hurts like a surgical operation. And re-thinking hurts again. Bultmann represents the hurt of demythologization and the new quest for the meaning that lies at the heart of the narratives: the resurrection is the meaning, the positive aspect, in the suffering of a life given, on the cross and in death. It is a word of life that transcends death. And Marxsen, in a more practical step forward, contextualizes this meaning and this dignity in the mission of the crucified who continues living, brought back to life in the mission of those who follow him. Nevertheless, the *myth* of resurrection cannot be reduced to understanding of its meaning and continuity of mission.

Continuing with the reading of Ricouer, the *myth* 'makes us feel': it helps us to work out diffuse and conflicting feelings, above all despairing feelings. The resurrection integrates the feeling of mourning with that of surprise, a surprise that mourning, on its own, would not be able to integrate. It is a feeling that does not derive from mourning itself. And this means that it needs a new language, beyond mourning. It is, in effect, a question of an 'experience' that brings newness with new feelings, to which I shall return shortly. But the *myth* also 'makes us act': it guides us to new modes of action, which involves breaks, in the sense of a practical and present form of death and new life. Faced with Peter's announcement, the first reaction of the crowd, which felt responsible for the death of the righteous one and felt itself facing the judgment of the One who raised him – 'this man . . . you crucified . . . But God raised him up' – was to ask the question, 'Brothers, what should we do?' (Acts 2.23–4, 37). Killed and raised up *to live a new life*: here, in Part 3 of this issue, the requirements of a raised-up and raising-up life in practice are set out. And, finally, the *myth* 'makes us hope': it opens or strengthens or reforms or transfigures horizons and journeys in the landscape of human existence. Hence the insistence on the dialectic between the resurrection of the dead and the resurrection of Jesus as respectively horizon and event.

II. The experience of resurrection

For the Andeans portrayed here (Irarrazabal), whose main life-experience is 'rising-on-death', mixing feasting with tears, the vague concept of life after death is insufficient: it needs to be celebrated with meals and rituals surrounding the dead, an experience through the bodily feelings of communion in the midst of life in which some are for others the heart of life, medium and mediators, intercessors of life. The experience of resurrection in memory, in the collective memory, in invocation and in blessing, ultimately in a 'communion of saints' that has a life-giving power, opens our eyes to this virtually universal fact among the human race: resurrection is not a doctrine of the highest dignity, nor is it a language with sublime meaning; it is an experience.

The language of the texts shows us that the experience of Jesus' disciples was one of the most complete surprise: they did not 'discover' – as one does in scientific discoveries – but their eyes were opened, in the passive, and they 'underwent' a vision, an experience. And even when they had seen Jesus in the state proper to God, they did not have an experience of divinity. As in the memory of Israel, it was a matter of the 'divine passive': the God of the Bible systematically refuses to make a spectacle of himself by arrogating the narcissistic state of idol to himself but, on the contrary, reveals something more than himself to the benefit of those who accept his pure gift. It was a matter of experience of the humanity of Jesus in the glory of God, the one humbled on the cross now raised up into *Lord* and *Firstborn* in order to share his path of glorified humanity with the humanity of the humbled. This experience sits decisively at the root of the language. Only in this way is the language not rigidified into a myth that would rather mask reality and deceive hope. When we move from language and announcement to experience, then language fulfils its true *mythic* function. And, in our case, it is not a matter of any sort of experience, but the experience of many new relationships.

III. The relationships of resurrection

What is most noticeable in the language and appreciable in the experience of Jesus' resurrection and in communion with the dead is, undoubtedly, the fact of relationships that are surprisingly new and stronger than death. Even for Jesus himself, his resurrection – glorification, lifting up, exaltation – is something he 'receives' as gift in response to his obedience. It begins in the hidden source of the heart of God, the mystery of and design for life in God. In this the Father is engaged as primary source, the Spirit as life-force, and the Son himself as obedience and continuity of mission, receiving in order to give: for Jesus, as risen Lord, it is a matter of continuity of mission, of his messianism without narcissism, till the glorification of the New Heavens and New Earth, a glorification that consists of the fullness of the resurrection of the dead. Therefore, from the *mythic* language that, for God's part, proclaims Jesus' resurrection to the *mythic* language that, still for God's part, proclaims the eschatological horizons of the New Heavens and New Earth as a New Jerusalem inhabited by a new humanity. A city of open doors, of communal living, made of meadow and no longer of temples and sacrifices – all this is made possible by a creative and contagious world of *new relationships*.

Resurrection is something that is received as gift, and which is given with the same freedom as thankfulness. It is not won; it is not deserved; it is not a right – it is not natural. It is the most complete experience of grace, of salvation by grace. And it is entire grace because it is entire salvation and not just that of a 'soul' – which would be salvation of what had not been lived, in Moltmann's apt expression. It is not enough to speak of the resurrection *of the flesh*. This can be transfigured only in the transfiguration of the heavens and earth into the New Heavens and New Earth, in true and creaturely holy communion, the Communion of Saints. Now, if human beings are, basically, a knot of relationships, the resurrection comes about in these relationships, which transfigure what it means to be human. It is anticipated in the hospitality of Abraham, whose bosom is made wide enough to gather in the poor man Lazarus. Mary Magdalen, accepted in the Master's hospitality, becomes the bearer of the news, giving what she received.

Relationships are, then, the setting for the possible experience of resurrection, the setting for its anticipation – for the *prolepsis* – and for its power of resistance, of insurrection. Relationships *from others and toward others* are also the space of its *eschatological reserve*. Relationships are the place of memory and of collective com-memoration, of the youthful freshness of wonderment, of the laying-down and synthesis of wisdom, and of courageous action for the sake of the future. Finally, resurrection, on account of the way it receives and forms new relationships, is an absolute victory because it is victory without producing vanquished, drawing into its bosom, through forgiveness and through the newness of its relationships, even executioners and enemies, even death itself, transforming it from the great enemy into our servant.

Perhaps the best language we have today in which to speak of and experience the resurrection of the dead, after modern criticism and in the face of modern problems, is the language and experience of *new relationships*, in many directions, with the dead, with the earth, with strangers – in short, with others.

Translated by Paul Burns

Notes

1. J. Sobrino, 1999, *La fe en Jesucristo: Ensayo desde las víctimas*, Madrid: Trotta (Eng. trans., 2001, *Christ the Liberator: A View from the Victims*, Maryknoll, NY: Orbis).
2. Cf. P. Tillich, 1952, *The Courage to Be*, New York: Charles Scribner's Sons; O. Cullmann, 'Immortality of the Soul or Resurrection from the Dead. The Witness of the New Testament', in K. Stendahl (ed.), 1965, *Immortality and Resurrection*, New York: MacMillan.

DOCUMENTATION

I. Migration from Africa to Spain

RAFAEL LARA

In the months of May and June 2006 the number of immigrants from Black Africa to Spain increased. This section of the *Documentation* for this issue provides an analysis of the tragedy of clandestine immigration and the Spanish government's 'Africa Plan'.

Africa Plan, Rabat summit, and migratory 'crisis'

The drama of migration is becoming more pronounced. Approximately three thousand people have died in the last six months on the route from Africa to the Canary Islands. The number of victims of clandestine immigration is increasing at a horrifying rate.

There is nothing casual about this situation. The migration policies of the Spanish government – border controls and closed frontiers, laws on 'aliens' that prevent immigration in practice, repatriation and links with security – are now leading directly to this result.

The scenarios of the drama have shifted inexorably as difficulties of breaching border controls have increased: from Cadiz to Granada and Almería, then to Ceuta, Melilla, and Morocco. And lately as far as the Sahara, Mauritania, and now Senegal.

The routes are now much longer (1,500 kms from Mauritania; double that from Senegal) and more dangerous, but at the same time they have become cheaper owing to larger embarkation vessels (dugout canoes) and reduced mafia involvement.

Faced with the increase in numbers, the government has responded by tightening the screw still further in the direction followed over recent years: more border controls and closures, reliance above all on police actions, even involving the army, repatriation, and pressure on countries of origin or transit of migrants.

(i) The scale of the tragedy

It is impossible to obtain accurate figures on the scale of the drama afflicting the African coasts on the migration route to the Canaries over the past six months.

According to the government, some eight thousand people arrived in the Canary Islands on rafts and in dugouts over the first five months of 2006, almost doubling the number of people intercepted during the whole of 2005. At the same time it is very difficult to discover, even approximately, how many lost their lives trying to emigrate from the Sahara, Mauritania, and now Senegal.

On 20 March the government acknowledged that the CNI (National Intelligence Centre) had alerted it to the massive number (between 1,200 and 1,700) of immigrant deaths during the months of November and December 2005; these figures have been collected by the Civil Guard from December on and, according to Ministry of Defence (which is responsible for the CNI), were secret and not for publication. The Mauritania Red Crescent had already used these figures to state at the beginning of March that between 1,200 and 1,300 immigrants had died in the previous six months trying to reach the Canary Island coasts from Africa. In May the Red Cross confirmed that since the start of the year the Atlantic waters separating the West African coast from the Canaries had swallowed 1,500 people.

According to the APDHA (Andalusian Association for Human Rights), at least 1,500 should be added for the first five months of 2006 to the between 1,200 and 1,700 who lost their lives in November and December of last year. This raises the number of people who have lost their lives on their way to the Canaries to around three thousand over the previous six months. We are looking at a human catastrophe on a vast scale.

(ii) The Africa Plan is not for Africa but serves EU interests

The Africa Plan has been sold by the government as a re-ordering of its foreign policy priorities, with the aim of establishing a new, deeper, and more global framework for its relations with sub-Saharan Africa. It is true that it has brought in some positive measures, since it begins to recognize the needs of the whole continent. But it is actually a plan conceived above all as a means of tackling European problems in relation to migrants – especially their control and rejection.

The aspect of cooperation is linked to the global reach of the plan, which means control of migration by the originating countries. The struggle against poverty it claims to promote is attached to measures that fall very far short of the requirements imposed by the gravity of the situation. As an example, the sum of 400 million euros allotted for 2006 is a drop in the ocean, the equivalent of building a bridge over the Bay of Cadiz. Much of the aid listed is destined for international organizations (world bodies rather than specifically African ones, such as Global Fund for the Fight against AIDS, the 'Quick Way' Education for All Initiative, the UN Fund for Emergency Relief, and so on) and had already been budgeted.

As they had to be, the various aid projects are presented as matters related to development for Africa. But they are this only to a relative extent, since in reality they promote Spanish fishing interests or security of energy supply, promoting participation in 'opportunities' in the hydrocarbons sector (*sic*; no comment).

Besides this, the bulk of the measures set out in the Africa Plan, and the most specific of them, are designed to strengthen migration control and to force African nations to control their emigration. Suffice to list the declared objectives:

(a) increasing the number of Interior Attachés at embassies and consulates in certain countries;
(b) measures of control at Spanish borders;
(c) means of obtaining information about routes followed and methods used by the networks (assigned to the CNI);
(d) strengthening means of immediate repatriation of illegal immigrants;
(e) completing the network of agreements for collaboration on migration and re-admission;
(f) drawing multilateral organizations and institutions into the task of working to prevent illegal immigration, both from Africa and from the EU.

So that justice may be seen to be done, there is a little postscript added to point (b): *to encourage measures tending to the integration of immigrant communities.* A somewhat insubstantial postscript, which imposes very little in the way of obligation but attempts, unsuccessfully, to embellish the whole.

(iii) The Euro-Africa Conference on Migration and Development, Rabat, July 2006

The trend to increased police activity and repression has been further accentuated by the plan presented in Dakar on 7 June by a Spanish-French-Moroccan consortium. This plan was in turn approved at the Euro-Africa

Conference on Migration and Development held in Rabat on 10–11 July.

The real objective of this Conference was precisely to control the flow of migrants. Despite the fact that the Plan cited above had the headline intention of encouraging development in originating or transit countries, and that it proposed several measures that can on principle appear positive (such as cutting the cost of sending remittances and encouraging this saving to be put to productive use or used to create small businesses . . .), the fact is that such positive measures, as Prof. Medhi Lalou has said, are not specified or budgeted, which makes their execution doubtful.

Algeria was a harsh critic of this Conference, on the grounds that the valid interlocutor would have been the African Union, not a selection of countries putting forward European strategies. Consequently, it refused to take part.

In practice, this major initiative on the part of the Spanish government, backed by the EU and most strongly by France, was a further insistence on more of the same: to prevent immigrants entering the country by any means possible, to return those who succeed, and above all to put pressure on the poorest countries in Africa to 'prevent the emigration of their citizens'. In this way, they are requiring them to commit a clear violation of the Human Rights Charter. Or does the Universal Declaration on Human Rights not say (art. 13): 'Everyone has the right to leave any country, including his own, and to return to his country'?

Translated by Paul Burns

II. Migration from the Americas and Caribbean

ALBERTO LOPEZ PULIDO

The continual movement and migration of people between what has become Latin and Central America, Mexico, and the Caribbean in relation to the United States represent an integral human part of the history of the Americas. Between 1990 and 2000 the numbers of immigrants coming from these countries into the United States have increased significantly, with the largest increase being from Mexico at an impressive 130 per cent. In fact, according to some studies, over half of the households in the Mexican State of Zacatecas have personal ties with someone in the United States. Immigration from Latin America has increased by 86 per cent; from Central America by 79 percent; and from the Caribbean by 52 per cent.

Prior to European contact with the Americas, indigenous groups presented a history of movement and migration with the objective of preserving and reproducing their culture and traditions. This is captured beautifully by the contemporary Mexican writer Miguel Méndez, who in his novel *Peregrinos de Aztlán* describes this movement as a cyclical pilgrimage where pilgrims, anointed by the spirit of the ancient gods, are guided to their original homeland, which is now situated within the deserts of the United States. He describes them as a proud and nomadic race with their feet wounded by centuries of pilgrimage, who symbolize marginalized and oppressed immigrants who because of their historical ties to the land acquire citizenship and receive justice.

The history of these interdependent regions reveals a historical past of expansionism and imperialism guided by the political and economic interests of Europe and the United States. As a result, these acts of migration and movement for the majority of these nations represent unique political acts of entering and violating borders in politically-charged regions that were once part of these communities' histories and legacies. These contemporary acts of movement are the result of economic and political policies by the elite, which have devastated nations and small communities through lack of economic resources, as a result of war or persecution, or by people seeking asylum. The main objective of these contemporary pilgrims is identical to those of their ancestors: to preserve and reproduce their cultural traditions in an attempt to reaffirm their self-worth and human dignity. Unfortunately, in the contemporary world such human expressions have become clandestine acts within forbidden spaces. This relates directly to the structural violence against the most vulnerable, who continue to be exploited.

The forbidden space of the U.S.-Mexico border has become a war-zone with government-sanctioned border enforcement through programmes such as Operation Gatekeeper, the deployment of the National Guard, and the installation of high-tech surveillance in an attempt to maintain 'homeland security' and protect the country from terrorists in a post-9/11 United States. This has had a devastating impact on the human rights of immigrants. Unlike the European immigrants, who were welcomed with open arms by the US government, we are instead faced with the gruesome reality of the rising death toll of immigrants as they are forced into the deserts and mountains in an attempt to enter the United States successfully from Mexico and other Central and Latin American countries. The loss of life as a result of such policies is placed at approximately 3,600 migrants, with little being done to change this reality.

A response to a coordinated effort of organizing thousands of Latino immigrant groups who seek just and humane immigration policies has been the steady rise of anti-immigrant vigilante groups such as the Minutemen or *Los caza-inmigrantes* (immigrant-hunters). They have incorporated tactics that seek to intimidate women and men who seek employment by photographing and videotaping their every move. Their tactics are extreme and help fuel the anti-immigrant and xenophobic attitude against Latino immigrants. The response by the community has been to create pan-Latino coalitions throughout all the major cities in the United States demanding the enforcement of immigrants' human rights by appropriate law enforcement agencies and officials. At present, there is an emerging movement to establish numerous sanctuary cities for immigrants such as Houston, Texas; Baltimore, Maryland; and Boston, Massachusetts. The goals of sanctuary cities are to reaffirm the rights of immigrants and treat them with the dignity that they deserve.

Another very important issue related to immigration to the United States from the Americas is the social and cultural challenges it is creating in certain countries. Immigration has resulted in uprooting thousands of adult men and an increasing number of women, which has wreaked havoc on many families. According to the Mexican cultural anthropologist Olivia

Ruiz, 60 percent of households in Mexico are being led by a single head of household, the majority of whom are women. This has major implications for the traditional Mexican family structure in terms of the feminization of poverty and the impact of truancy, drug use, depression, and suicide among young people. Owing to the difficulty of attaining legal residence in the United States and the risk of crossing the border, the reunification of families represents a critical problem for years to come.

Economic and political interdependence has been firmly established as a result of US political and economic policies in their historical relations with Latin and Central American nations, the Caribbean, and Mexico. The best contemporary example is the emergence of remittances, popularly known as *migradolares*, which accounts for nations receiving dollars from citizens living abroad. Mexico leads the way, having received over $20 billion last year, with proportionately impressive figures for Central and Latin American nations and the Caribbean. While such figures are impressive in terms of the capital they provide these nations – such monies are short-term solutions for the systemic problems found in these countries – they actually place the future of development for these nations on the shoulders of the most vulnerable.

Migration and movement do not occur in a vacuum, but within a physical and geographical place. Hence, a sensible understanding of migration in the Americas requires a careful historical analysis of this ever-changing region. We must recognize that the border region in the United States is a recent phenomenon within a larger history. It began as vast territories for a range of distinct living indigenous communities. It was then transformed into a colonial possession for the Spanish empire for three hundred years. This emerging *Mestizo* region then became northern Mexico for a short period, before being colonized by American westward expansion with economic and political interests along the Pacific Ocean. The recent history is one of NAFTA and free trade for the economic elite. The numerous past centuries have been ones of continual change and transformation. It is certain that this region will continue to change with the movement and migration of Latin American people at its centre.

Contributors

DR MARCELLA ALTHAUS-REID is an Argentine theologian and a reader in Christian ethics and theology in the School of Divinity, University of Edinburgh, Scotland. Her many publications include *Indecent Theology. Theological Perversions in Sex, Gender and Politics* (2001); *The Queer God* (2003); *From Feminist Theology to Indecent Theology* (2005); and *Liberation Theology and Sexuality* (2006).

Address: Faculty of Divinity, New College, University of Edinburgh, Mound Place, Edinburgh EH1 2LX, Scotland
E-mail: althausm@staffmail.ed.ac.uk

GIUSEPPE BARBAGLIO was born in Crema (Cremona) in Italy in 1934 and is a layman living in Rome. He taught at the Interregional Theological Faculty in Milan and is managing editor of the 'Bible in History'series for Edizioni Dehoniane in Bologna and also (with R. Penna) 'Texts of the Christian Origins'. His main publications are *Paolo di Tarso e le origini cristiane* (^{3}2002); *La laicità del credente: Interpretazione biblica* (1987); *Dio violento? Lettura delle Scritture ebraiche e cristiane* (1991); *La prima lettera ai Corinzi* (^{2}2005); *Teologia di Paolo: Abbozzi in forma epistolare* (^{2}2001); *Gesù ebreo di Galilea: Indagine storica* (^{4}2003); *Il pensare dell'apostolo Paolo* (^{2}2005); *Gesù di Nazaret Paolo di Tarso: Confronto storico* (2006).

Address: Via del Pellegrino 113, 00186 Roma, Italy
E-mail: giuseppebarbaglio@libero.it

PEDRO CASALDÁLIGA is a Catalan, born in Balsareny in 1928. He was ordained priest in Barcelona in 1952. From 1971 to 2004 he was bishop of the diocese of São Félix do Araguaia (Brazil). His published works include: *Clamor elemental* (1971); *Tierra nuestra, Libertad* (1974); *Cantigas menores* (1979); *Misa de la tierra sin males* (1980); *Poemas e autos sacramentais sertanejos* (1982);

Fuego e ceniza al viento (1984); *El tiempo y la espera* (1986); *Me llamarán subversivo* (1987); *Todavía estas palabras* (1990); *Llena de dios y tan nuestra* (1991); and, with José-María Vigil, *Espiritualidad de la Liberación* (1993; Eng. trans. *The Spirituality of Liberation*, 1994).

Address: Caixa postal 5, São Félix do Araguaia, MT, Brazil 78670.000

MÁRCIO FABRI DOS ANJOS was born in Brazil in 1943 and researches and teaches Bioethics at the São Camilo University Faculty; he also teaches theology at the Faculty of Our Lady of the Assumption and at the São Paulo Institute of Higher Studies. He is a director member of the Brazilian Society of Bioethics and ex-president of the Brazilian Society of Theology and Religious Sciences. He has been managing editor of *Teología y nuevos paradigmas* (1999); *Vescovi per la speranza del mondo* (2001); *Novas Gerações e Vida Religiosa* (2004), and is author of 'Power and Vulnerability: A contribution of developing countries to the ethical debate on genetics', in L. S. Cahill (ed.), *Genetics, Theology, Ethics. An interdisciplinary conversation* (2005), and of numerous articles

Address: Rua Oliveira Alves, 164, 04210-060 São Paulo-SP, Brazil

DIEGO IRARRAZAVAL was born in Chile in 1942 and is a priest of the Congregation of the Holy Cross. He has been director of the Institute of Aymara Studies and has worked in indigenous pastoral care in Peru and other places on the continent. From 2001 to 2006 he was president of EATWOT (Association of Third-World Theologians). He is the author of *Religión del pobre y liberación* (1978); *Teología en la fe del pueblo* (1992); *Inculturación* (1998); *Raíces de la esperanza* (2004); *Gozar la espiritualidad* (2004); *Gozar la ética* (2005). At present he collaborates in parish pastoral work in Santiago, and he directs the Holy Cross education programme in Chile.

Address: Casilla 238, Correo 11, Santiago, Chile
E-mail: diegoira@hotmail.com

ALBERTO LOPEZ PULIDO is director and professor of ethnic studies and associate director of the Center for the Study of Latino Catholicism at what he calls the 'frontier' University of San Diego. He is the author of numerous publications focusing on the intersection of race, religion, and community.

His most recent publications include a study of Catholic social teaching and ethnic studies in Catholic higher education and a book on the *Penitentes* of New Mexico. He is currently working on a collaborative comparative study on the sacred expression of Mexican immigrants in San Diego and New York City.

Address: Ethnic Studies Program, University of San Diego, 5998 Alcala Park, San Diego, CA 92110, USA

JÜRGEN MOLTMANN was born in Hamburg in 1926 and is a member of the German Evangelical-Reformed Church. He studied and took further degrees in theology at Göttingen University. From 1958 to 1963 he was professor at the Wuppertal Ecclesiastical College; from 1963 to 1967 professor of systematic theology at Bonn University; he is currently professor emeritus of systematic theology at Tübingen University and has been Chair of the 'Evangelical Theology Association'. His publications translated into English include *Theology of Hope* (1967); *The Crucified God* (1973); *The Church in the Power of the Spirit* (1975); *The Trinity and the Kingdom: the Doctrine of God* (1981); *God in Creation* (1985); *The Way of Jesus Christ* (1989); *The Spirit of Life: A Universal Affirmation* (1992); *The Coming of God* (1996); *The Source of Life* 1997); *Science and Wisdom* (2003); *In the End the Beginning* (2004).

Address: Biesinger Strasse 25, D-72070 Tübingen, Germany

KARL-HEINZ OHLIG was born on 15 September 1938. He holds a doctorate in theology. In 1970 he was appointed professor of Catholic theology and the teaching of Catholic theology at the Saar College of Education. Since 1978 he has held the chair of religious science and the history of Christianity at the Saar University. He is head of the Religious Science Workshop.

Address: Universität des Saarlandes, P.O. Box No. 151150, D-66041 Saarbrücken, Germany; private address: Vorstadtstrasse. 13, D-66117 Saarbrücken, Germany.

THOMAS SCHÄRTL was born in 1969 in Vohenstrauss (Bavaria). He studied in Regensburg, Munich, Tübingen, and Münster and holds a doctorate in theology from the Eberhard-Karls-University of Tübingen and an M.A. in philosophy from the Jesuit Munich School of Philosophy. He has lectured at the Universities of Regensburg and Münster, at the School of Catholic Theology in Paderborn, and since 2006 has been assistant professor at the CUA in Washington, DC. His areas of research include Trinitarian theology, the concept of God and divine attributes, religious epistemology, philosophy of language, hermeneutics, eschatology, and metaphysics.

Address: School of Theology and Religious Studies, Caldwell Hall, Catholic University of America, Washington, DC 20064

JON SOBRINO was born in the Basque Country in 1938 and educated in Spain, Germany, and the USA, from where he holds a Master's Degree in Engineering. He joined the Society of Jesus in 1956 and has sine 1957 belonged to the Central American Province and lived mainly in El Salvador. He is professor of theology and director of the Mgr Romero Centre at the Catholic University of Central America in San Salvador. He is joint editor with Ignacio Ellacuría, the Rector of the university, murderd in 1993, of *Mysterium Liberationis: Fundamental Concepts of Liberation Theology* (1993). Among his more recent publications translated into English are the two-volume christology *Jesus the Liberator* (1993) and *Christ the Liberator* (2001).

Address: Centro Monseñor Romero/UCA, apartado 01-106, San Salvador, El Salvador.
E-mail: jsobrino@cmr.uca.edu.sv

LUIZ CARLOS SUSIN is professor of systematic theology at the Pontifical Catholic University of Rio Grande do Sul and at the Higher School of Theology and Franciscan Spirituality, both in Porto Alegre, Brazil. He is an ex-president of the Brazilian Society for Theology and Religious Studies, and secretary general of the World Forum for Theology and Liberation. His recent research has been into the relationship between theology and ecology. His publications include *A Criação de Deus* (2003); *Deus, Pai, Filho e Espírito Santo; Jesus, Filho de Deus e Filho de Maria; Assim na terra como no céu*, some published by Paulinas (São Paulo) and some by Vozes (Petrópolis).

Address: Rua Juarez Távora 171, 91529–100 Porto Alegre, Brazil

ANDRÉS TORRES QUEIRUGA was born in 1940 and holds doctorates in philosophy from the University of Santiago de Compostela and in theology from the Gregorian in Rome. He taught fundamental theology at the Theological

Institute in Santiago from 1968 to 1987 and is currently professor of philosophy of religion at the university there. He is editor of *Encrucillada: Revista Galega de Pensamento Cristián*, as well as being on the editorial board of *Iglesia Viva*, an adviser to *Revista Portuguesa de Filosofía*, and a founding member of the Spanish Society of Religious Studies. His many published works include *La revelación de Dios en la realización del hombre* (1977, trans. into Italian, Portuguese, and German), *Creo en Dios Padre* (^{5}1998), *El problema de Dios en la modernidad* (1998), *Fin del cristianismo premoderno* (200), *Repensar la resurrección* (2203), and *Esperanza a pesar del mal* (2005).

Address: Facultad de Filosofía, Campus Sur, 1748 Santiago de Compostela, Spain
E-mail: atorres@usc.es

SENÉN VIDAL was born in 1941 and presented his doctoral thesis at the Pontifical University of Salamanca in 1979, publishing it in 1982 under the title *La resurrección de Jesús en las cartas de Pablo. Análisis de las tradiciones*. He has lectured on the New Testament in several universities and theological centres in Spain, Mexico, and Venezuela. He is currently professor of New Testament studies at the Augustinian Study Centre in Valladolid. His more recent works include *Los tres proyectos de Jesús y el cristianismo naciente. Un ensayo de reconstrucción histórica* (2003); *El proyecto mesiánico de Pablo* (2005); *Jesús el Galileo* (2006); *El primer escrito cristiano. Texto bilingüe de 1 Tesalonicenses con introducción y comentario* (2006).

Address: Plaza de Colón, 15, 37001 Salamanca, Spain
E-mail: senenvi@jazzfree.com; senenvi@gmail.com

CONCILIUM

FOUNDERS
Anton van den Boogaard
Paul Brand
Yves Congar, OP†
Hans Küng
Johann-Baptist Metz
Karl Rahner, SJ†
Edward Schillebeeckx

FOUNDATION BOARD
Jan Peters SJ (President)
Paul Vos (Treasurer)
Erik Borgman
Susan Ross
Felix Wilfred

DIRECTORS
Regina Ammicht-Quinn (Frankfurt, Germany)
Maria Clara Bingemer (Rio de Janeiro, Brazil)
Erik Borgman (Nijmegen, The Netherlands)
Lisa Sowle Cahill (Boston, USA)
Eamonn Conway (Limerick, Ireland)
Dennis Gira (Paris, France)
Hille Haker (Frankfurt, Germany)
Diego Irarrazaval (Santiago, Chile)
Solange Lefebvre (Montreal, Canada)
Daniel Marguerat (Lausanne, Switzerland)
Eloi Messi Metogo (Yaoundé, Cameroon)
Paul D. Murray (Durham, UK)
Susan Ross (Chicago, USA)
Silvia Scatena (Reggio Emilia, Italy).
Jon Sobrino SJ (San Salvador, El Salvador)
Luiz Carlos Susin (Porto Alegre, Brazil)
Andrés Torres Queiruga (Santiago de Compostela, Spain)
Marie-Theres Wacker (Münster, Germany)
Elaine Wainwright (Auckland, New Zealand)
Felix Wilfred (Madras, India)

PUBLISHERS
SCM-Canterbury Press (London, UK)
Matthias-Grünewald-Verlag/ Der Schwabenverlag (Ostfildern, Germany)
Editrice Queriniana (Brescia, Italy)
Editorial Verbo Divino (Estella, Spain)
Editora Vozes (Petrópolis, Brazil)

General Secretariat: Erasmusplein 1, 6525 HT Nijmegen, The Netherlands
http://www.concilium.org
Manager: Baroness Christine van Wijnbergen

Concilium Subscription Information

February 2007/1: *Theology and Religious Pluralism*

April 2007/2: *The Land*

June 2007/3: *AIDS*

October 2007/4: *Christianity and Democracy*

December 2007/5: *Ages of Life and Christian Experience*

New subscribers: to receive *Concilium 2007* (five issues) anywhere in the world, please copy this form, complete it in block capitals and send it with your payment to the address below.

Please enter my subscription for *Concilium 2007*

Individuals
____ £40.00 UK
____ £60.00 overseas
____ $110.00 North America/Rest of World
____ €99.00 Europe

Institutions
____ £55.00 UK
____ £75.00 overseas
____ $140 North America/Rest of World
____ €125.00 Europe

Postage included – airmail for overseas subscribers

Payment Details:
Payment must accompany all orders and can be made by cheque or credit card
I enclose a cheque for £/$/€ _____ Payable to SCM-Canterbury Press Ltd
Please charge my Visa/MasterCard (Delete as appropriate) for £/$/€ _____
Credit card number ....
Expiry date ....
Signature of cardholder ....
Name on card ....
Telephone .... E-mail ....

Send your order to *Concilium*, SCM-Canterbury Press Ltd
9–17 St Albans Place, London N1 ONX, UK
Tel +44 (0)20 7359 8033 Fax +44 (0)20 7359 0049
E-Mail: office@scm-canterburypress.co.uk

Customer service information:
All orders must be prepaid. Subscriptions are entered on an annual basis (i.e. January to December). No refunds on subscriptions will be made after the first issue of the Journal has been despatched. If you have any queries or require information about other payment methods, please contact our Customer Services department.

www.ingramcontent.com/pod-product-compliance
Lightning Source LLC
Chambersburg PA
CBHW070643300426
44111CB00013B/2239